Greatest Texas Sports Stories You've Never Heard

The Greatest Texas Sports Stories You've Never Heard

Al Pickett

Foreword by Dave Campbell

State House Press

McMurry University
Abilene, Texas

Library of Congress Cataloging-in-Publication Data

Pickett, Al.
   The greatest Texas sports stories you've never heard /
   Al Pickett; foreword by Dave Campbell.
       p. cm.
   Includes index.
   ISBN-13: 978-1-933337-17-3 (pbk.: alk. paper)
   ISBN-10: 1-933337-17-6 (pbk.: alk. paper)
1. University of Texas at Austin–Football–History. 2. Texas
Longhorns (Football team)–History. I. Title.

GV956.T47P53 2007
796.332'630976431--dc22

                                                        2007037525

State House Press
McMurry Station, Box 637
Abilene, TX 79697-0637
(325) 572-3974
(325) 572-3991 fax
www.mcwhiney.org/press

Distributed by Texas A&M University Press Consortium
1-800-826-8911 • www.tamu.edu/upress

Printed in the United States of America

ISBN-13: 978-1-933337-17-3
ISBN-10: 1-933337-17-6
10 9 8 7 6 5 4 3 2 1

Book designed by Rosenbohm Graphic Design

Dedication

To Carole, for her love and support

Table of Contents

Photos

Foreword

For me, reading Al Pickett's excellent book *The Greatest Texas Sports Stories You've Never Heard* was like taking a delightful trip down memory lane. And what I especially liked is the way he has covered the waterfront, providing readers with some stories about famous sports figures, but others about the not-so-famous. He has stories about a variety of sports and not just football or baseball or basketball—a fine mixture, you might say.

A number of the incidents touched on in the book I knew about. For some of them I had actually been a first-hand observer. But Pickett has supplied background and detail that expands and rounds out the incident, that supplies "the rest of the story."

An example: October 16, 1976, the Baylor Bears traveled to College Station to take on Emory Bellard's Texas Aggies. Baylor coach Grant Teaff had a good team that season. The season had opened in a memorable way: Baylor at home playing the Houston Cougars in the game that would mark the debut of coach Bill Yeoman's Cougars as a new member of the Southwest Conference. Baylor was favored but Houston won decisively, 23-5, and went on to win both the SWC crown and the Cotton Bowl game against unbeaten Maryland.

But Baylor was able to shake off that first-game disappointment and win its next four games, against Auburn, Illinois, South Carolina and SMU. A&M, meanwhile, had defeated Virginia Tech and Kansas State, had stumbled against Houston but had defeated Illinois before losing to Texas Tech.

That brought us to the Baylor-A&M game. I was there that day in the Kyle Field press box to cover the game for the *Waco Tribune-*

Herald. It looked like a game of equals although the Aggies would have the home advantage. But it wasn't a nip-and-tuck affair at all. A&M kicker Tony Franklin kicked a 64-yard field goal in the second quarter and then a 65-yarder in the third quarter—both records for field goal distance, or so we thought in the press box.

But before the day was over we found out differently. Ove Johansson, a native of Gothenburg, Sweden, and kicker for Abilene Christian University had picked that day to kick a 69-yarder, the longest field goal in football history. I remember getting the word before I left the press box that Johansson had actually upstaged Tony Franklin that day, but what I remember most is how upset Grant Teaff was that a long-range kicker had helped rip open a game the Aggies had won, 24-0, although six of their points came when they did not even drive across midfield.

Time proved I wasn't through with Tony Franklin. In 1994 a special committee of the Football Writers of America was named to select a Silver Anniversary All-America Team (meaning, the best collegians of the past 25 years). I was a member of that committee, representing the southwest, and when all the arguing had been done and the voting completed, three former Southwest Conference standouts had been chosen: offensive tackle Jerry Sisemore from Texas, linebacker Mike Singletary from Baylor, and kicker Tony Franklin from Texas A&M.

And Ove Johansson? How he happened to get from Gothenburg to Abilene, why he was so determined to kick a field goal for a record distance on October 16, 1976, and what has happened to him since, are all chronicled in Pickett's book. Interesting information, and good reading, too.

Another example: The first Cotton Bowl game I ever covered was played on January 1, 1954: Rice versus Alabama. I had just been named the new sports editor of the *Waco Tribune-Herald* following the death of my illustrious predecessor, H.H. (Jinx) Tucker. I had covered the Sugar Bowl game the previous year (Georgia Tech versus Ole Miss) but this was different. This was *the* Cotton Bowl.

Twice-beaten Rice was ranked No. 8 in the country and had just done a number (41-19) on Baylor in winding up its regular season. It had done so in no small part because of the terrific play of its superb junior, Dicky Maegle. I helped cover that Rice-Baylor game, and was eager to see more of Maegle, who was rapidly closing in on superstar status.

I saw a lot more of him that Cotton Bowl game than I expected. My first Cotton Bowl game became one of the most memorable Cotton Bowl games in history, Maegle rushing for a bowl-record 265 yards on just 11 carries, scoring on runs of 79, 95 and 34 yards. But it was that 95-yarder that stamped this Cotton Bowl game as unforgettable. Running free down the east sideline, Maegle appeared long gone for a touchdown when an Alabama player named Tommy Lewis came off the bench, threw a block into Maegle's blind side and knocked him to the ground. The crowd was transfixed. The press box was stunned—so were the officials. Referee Cliff Shaw hesitated, then signaled a Rice touchdown.

And so it was, officially.

Later, in explaining himself, Tommy Lewis said he couldn't help himself, he was "just too full of 'Bama." It's all there in Al Pickett's book, as you would expect.

I owe a debt of gratitude to Dicky Maegle for making my first Cotton Bowl one I could never forget. But I owe him even more. Years later, *Texas Football Magazine* ran a series of back-cover advertisements sponsored by Coca-Cola, with each ad honoring a legendary player from a Southwest Conference school. The player we selected from Texas A&M was John Kimbrough, the All-America fullback on A&M's 1939 national champions. Before preparing the series of ads, we wrote a letter to each of the players chosen, explained what we wanted to do, and asked them to give us written permission to use their name and likeness in the ad.

Kimbrough sent us a signed letter giving us his approval. So did all the other players who were being spotlighted. Later, after the Coke ad featuring an artist's drawing of Kimbrough in action in his heyday at A&M had been published, he sued us and Coca-Cola for one million dollars, claiming that in signing the letter he had not realized he was giving us permission to use his name. The case finally wound its way to court and a Dallas jury voted for us unanimously. That was after Dicky Maegle (and several of the other chosen players) had flown to Dallas and testified on our behalf. It became a landmark case for such things. You can look it up.

So, no, I never will forget Dicky Maegle.

A third example. Al Pickett offers a fascinating look at Sam Baugh in what some might call his senior citizen years. That devoted Texas rancher, committed golfer, and former outstanding football player Sam Baugh. "Slingin' Sammy Baugh," they called him.

Here's what I especially remember about Sam Baugh. In 1969, college football celebrated its Centennial Year, and as part of that celebration the NCAA asked the Football Writers Association of America to select an All-Time All-America Football Team. The players chosen then would be flown to New York and would be introduced and honored at a spotlighted banquet. The former presidents of the FWAA would comprise the selection committee. As president of the FWAA that year, I got to be part of the process.

We met at a hotel in Chicago to select the team. I went into the meeting expecting some of the fiercest arguments would involve the quarterback position, often the most publicized position on a football team. I was wrong. Almost by acclamation, those veteran football writers agreed Sammy Baugh had to be our man. Notre Dame's Johnny Lujack finished second.

In the subsequent press conference and banquet in New York, Baugh stole the show. He was the member of the team all the New York writers wanted to talk to. By then, he had been retired from professional football for more than twenty years, and from his All-America days at TCU for thirty-three years, but they hadn't forgotten him. Quite a guy, that Sammy Baugh.

Al Pickett has not overlooked *Texas Football Magazine* in his enjoyable book, and as founder of the magazine, I certainly appreciate his decision to include us and to report how and why the magazine came into being.

He also includes in his narrative a humorous account of a Dallas man, about to be married and leave on his honeymoon in Canada, who just couldn't wait to get a first copy of the magazine because he had to "have something to do there on my honeymoon." We sent him a magazine, of course.

Here's another little incident that transpired in the first year of the magazine. I received a letter one day from a man who said he was a convict in prison at Huntsville. He said he had always been a huge football fan, and his mother, knowing that, had mailed him a copy of this new "Texas Football" magazine she had found on a news stand.

He said he had taken the magazine with him to read while spending time in the prison library. While doing so, a commotion of some sort had broken out behind him, and he had turned around to see what all the fuss was about. When he turned back to resume his reading, he found someone had made off with his magazine.

"You just can't trust anybody down here," he said in his letter, and asked if I would please send him another. I did. Later on, he sent me a Christmas card which read: "From our house to your house."

I appreciated the gesture. And I think you will appreciate Al Pickett's collection of great Texas sports stories you've never heard. It deserves a place in every good sports library.

Dave Campbell
Founder, *Texas Football* magazine

Introduction

The popular American sport is called "football." But it has very little to do with feet. The sport is more about legs for running with the ball, arms for throwing the ball and hands for catching it.

Today, kickers are almost taken for granted, booting extra points with remarkable consistency and called on to kick field goals when offensive drives bog down on the opponents' end of the field. A good kicker is important, occasionally winning a game with a last-second boot.

But imagine being in scoring range once a team reaches mid-field. There was a time—albeit a very brief period—when kickers were putting it through the uprights with amazing accuracy from long distance.

When the 1976 football season began, the collegiate record for the longest field goal in a game was sixty-three yards. Joe Duren of Arkansas State had established the record on November 23, 1974, in a 22-20 victory over McNeese State. A year later—November 15, 1975—Fort Worth native Clark Kemble of Colorado State equaled the mark with a sixty-three-yard field goal in a 31-9 loss to Arizona.

Duren's and Kemble's sixty-three-yard efforts matched the NFL record that Tom Dempsey of the New Orleans Saints had set on November 8, 1970, in a 17-15 win over the Detroit Lions.

But all that changed on one remarkable day—October 16, 1976—when Texas A&M's Tony Franklin and Abilene Christian University's Ove Johansson broke the record three times within an hour or two of each other.

Collegiate kickers have broken the sixty-three-yard barrier only six other times since Franklin's and Johansson's record-setting afternoons in October of 1976. And four of the six long-distance feats came in either 1977 or 1978. Only a pair of kickers in Kansas—Tom Odle of Fort Hays State in 1988 and Martin Gramatica (who later kicked for the Dallas Cowboys) of Kansas State in 1998—have managed to put a kick through the uprights from that distance since 1978.

The Southwest Conference, better known for running backs such as Earl Campbell, was the center of the kicking universe in the golden age of collegiate kickers from 1976-1978. Franklin at A&M, Russell Erxleben of the University of Texas, and Steve Little of the University of Arkansas kicked excitement into football during that brief time.

But the long-distance record belongs to the most unlikely kicker imaginable, a Swedish-born soccer player who had never even kicked a field goal in an American football game until the 1976 season. A little more than a month later, Johansson booted his record-setting sixty-nine-yarder at Shotwell Stadium in Abilene on October 16, 1976.

Ten years later, I was in attendance for the anniversary of the record-setting kick. It was unimaginable as I saw Abilene Christian athletic director Wally Bullington—who was the Wildcats' coach in 1976—stand at the forty-one-yard line on the north end of Shotwell Stadium, the spot where Johansson had kicked his record.

I guess this book has been rattling around in my head ever since. How could someone kick a sixty-nine-yard field goal—and why doesn't anyone try it any more?

The story of how love led Johansson to Texas—and the record-setting field goal—is just one of many stories I hope readers will find interesting. This book is filled with other Texas sports stories, many that you may have never heard. Did you know that tragedy on that same day—October 16, 1976—changed University of Houston football coach Art Briles' life forever?

Did you know the greatest high school football coach in Texas history never played high school football himself? Or a case of déjà vu helped a Texan win the Masters golf championship?

It was a Texan who was eyewitness to two of the most memorable moments in World Series history. The last person to die in an NFL game was a Texan. It was a Texan who played an integral but forgotten role in the integration of baseball. The most unusual play in college football history occurred at the Cotton Bowl in Texas.

What about the wildest, wackiest finish to a high school football game ever? Yes, that happened in Texas, too. These are just some of the stories I've compiled in twenty-plus years covering Texas sports from the unique perspective of being a sports editor for the *Abilene Reporter-News* and a freelance writer for Dave Campbell's *Texas Football* magazine, *Total Texas Baseball* and *Red Raider Sports* magazines, as well as the play-by-play announcer for Abilene High School and Hardin-Simmons University football, basketball and baseball.

I hope you enjoy *The Greatest Texas Sports Stories You've Never Heard*. Hopefully, when you finish a chapter, you'll be able to say, "I didn't know that."

World's Longest Field Goal

What's love got to do with it? Everything, as far as Ove Johansson is concerned.

Eight years before Tina Turner recorded her 1984 hit "What's Love Got To Do With It," Johansson booted the longest field goal

Ove Johansson kicks the world's longest field goal.
Courtesy of Ove Johansson.

ever kicked in a football game at any level—high school, college or professional. His sixty-nine-yarder at Shotwell Stadium in Abilene on October 16, 1976, remains the world record today.

And love had everything to do it. Johansson, a native of Gothenburg, Sweden, who has made Amarillo his home for nearly thirty years now where he has his own investments firm, is perhaps the most unlikely person one could imagine to hold an American football record.

To understand what happened on that chilly autumn afternoon in Texas and the role it single-handedly played in causing a change in college football's rules, however, one must go back a few years earlier.

"We didn't have much money, and my dad had always encouraged me to go to the United States for a better opportunity," recalled Johansson, who said he was always active in all sports—soccer, ski jumping, and tennis, just to name a few—growing up in Sweden. "All I wanted to be was a P.E. (physical education) teacher."

Johansson said he joined the Swedish Navy, where he met a fellow seaman who was going to Texas to play semi-pro soccer with the Dallas Tornadoes. He invited Johansson to join him when his naval commitment was up, so Johansson came to Texas, settling in Irving.

"I played for a semi-pro soccer team in Dallas," Johansson recalled, "and I helped him organize the Irving Soccer Association. I also coached soccer."

It was during one of those soccer games in Irving that he saw a pretty girl—just a high school senior at the time—sitting in the stands. At halftime, Johansson got her phone number.

"Can you believe that?" he said, still laughing about his boldness more than thirty years later. "We dated for six months, but then my visa was up and I went back to Sweden."

During the time he was in the U.S., however, the soccer coach at Davis & Elkins, a small college in West Virginia, had seen Johansson play in a game in Colorado Springs. The coach at Davis & Elkins corresponded with Johansson back in Sweden and invited him to join that school's soccer team.

"I finally had to tell him that my dad didn't have six dollars in the bank, and I couldn't come unless I got a full scholarship," Johansson continued.

In the meantime, April, the pretty girl he had seen in the stands that day in Irving, came to Sweden in the summer of 1974 to meet Johansson's parents. While she was there, April informed Johansson that her father had taken a new job and her family was moving from Dallas to West Virginia. Then, a letter arrived from Davis & Elkins.

"I opened the letter, and it was an offer for a full scholarship to play soccer at Davis & Elkins," Johansson said. "So, I played soccer in the fall at Davis & Elkins in 1974."

There was only one problem, however. April wasn't in West Virginia with her family. She had enrolled in school at Abilene Christian College. So Johansson gave up his scholarship after one season at Davis & Elkins and transferred to Abilene Christian.

"I was starving to death," he said, "and I had no sports (Abilene Christian didn't have a soccer team). I didn't know if I could handle it."

Johansson said he went to the Wildcats' football games in the fall of 1975, but only because April was playing in the band. He didn't stay for the football game itself because he didn't understand the American football rules. Then in January of 1976, Johansson was walking back to his dorm room when he saw a guy kicking a football.

"I can do that," Johansson thought to himself, "so I started working out twice a day by myself. April would hold the ball for me."

Greg Stirman, a member of the Abilene Christian football team, saw Johansson working out and went in to tell head coach Wally Bullington about Johansson.

"I remember Greg Stirman coming into my office," Bullington recalled. "He said there is some Swede out there kicking the living daylights out of the ball."

Bullington invited Johansson to join the team, and he became the Wildcats' place-kicker in the fall of 1976, his only season of college football.

October 16, 1976, was already going to be a big day on the Abilene Christian campus. It was the school's first homecoming game as Abilene Christian University, having officially changed its name from Abilene Christian College that fall. ACU senior running back Wilbert Montgomery, who went on to a terrific professional career with the Philadelphia Eagles and later became an assistant coach for the St. Louis Rams, was poised to break the collegiate touchdown record that day, too. Montgomery's next touchdown would be his sixty-seventh, breaking the old mark of sixty-six held by Walter Payton of Jackson State.

"Wilbert came up to me that week in the cafeteria and said he was going to break the record Saturday against East Texas State on homecoming," Johansson added. "I said, 'What's homecoming?'"

Johansson then asked someone else in the cafeteria what the record was for the longest field goal. Sixty-three yards by Tom Dempsey of the New Orleans Saints, he was told.

"Ove came into my office that Friday," Bullington recalled, "and with that Swedish accent said, 'Coach, Wilbert is going to set a record tomorrow. I want to set a record, too.'"

Certainly a bold request for a kicker whose longest field goal to date in his first and only collegiate season was forty yards, but Bullington agreed to give Johansson a shot at the record if the opportunity presented itself.

Sure enough, Montgomery achieved his record as college football's most prolific scorer late in the second quarter when he turned a screen pass into a forty-three-yard scoring play and his sixty-seventh career touchdown. But his record was overshadowed by Johansson's long-distance accomplishment.

Johansson achieved his record earlier in the game—with 2:13 to go in the first quarter to be exact—although by the time he kicked it, the record was no longer sixty-three yards. Texas A&M and Baylor had kicked off an hour earlier in College Station, and the Aggies' barefooted Tony Franklin had booted a sixty-four-yard field goal in the second quarter. Bullington and Johansson both remember the announcement of Franklin's record kick being made by the public address announcer at Shotwell Stadium.

Here is how the hometown *Abilene Reporter-News* described the longest field goal in football history:

"Johansson, a former soccer player from Sweden, who had never kicked a field goal in his life until seven months ago, sent a sixty-nine-yarder through the south uprights of Shotwell Stadium with 2:13 left in the first quarter. The snap from center was a little high, but Johansson hit it perfectly and helped along by a sixteen-mile-per-hour wind, it cleared the bar, dropping to the ground some three yards past the uprights.

"The previously quiet crowd of 13,000 erupted in celebration and the Wildcat bench emptied onto the field, smothering Johansson with congratulations as the official raised his arms high in the air."

A few years ago, Johansson said he was attending an investments seminar in Dallas when a man approached him.

"I was on the East Texas State team that day you kicked the sixty-nine-yard field goal," the man told Johansson. "Do you remember what you did before the game?"

Johansson acknowledged that he remembered he and his holder Dean Low practiced field goals from seventy yards during pregame warmups.

"You were standing in the middle of our team while we were doing calisthenics," the man continued. "Do you remember what we did after you kicked one from seventy yards?"

"No, I guess I don't," Johansson replied.

"We went running to our coaches," the man said. "We said, 'They're going to kick a field goal if they get to the forty-yard line.'"

Oddly enough, Franklin bettered his NCAA record of sixty-four yards with a sixty-five-yarder in the third quarter of the Aggies' 24-0 win over Baylor. But neither kick—sandwiched around Johansson's that same day—counted as the longest field goal in football history. That record belonged to Johansson of Abilene Christian, which was a member of the NAIA at the time.

That amazing day in 1976 when there were three field goals longer than sixty-four yards kicked in the state of Texas sparked a national interest in long-distance field goals. The next year, Texas' Russell Erxleben kicked a sixty-seven-yarder against Rice to break Franklin's NCAA record. Two weeks later, Steve Little of Arkansas tied Erxleben's record with a sixty-seven-yard field goal against the Longhorns.

There have been seven field goals sixty-five yards or longer kicked in the history of college football. Four of them were kicked in the state of Texas in either 1976 or 1977.

Dave Campbell's *Texas Football* magazine featured Erxleben, who was from Seguin, and Franklin, who called Fort Worth home, on the cover of its 1978 magazine. It is the only time in the magazine's forty-seven-year history that kickers have graced the cover. The magazine headlined its feature story "It's Cannon Foot vs. Christmas Toe: A conversation with Texas A&M's Tony Franklin and Texas' Russell Erxleben, the two best college kickers in the whole wide world."

The 1978 season, however, marked a change in the rule and an end to the cross-country field goals. After Franklin and Johansson's performance on October 16, 1976, Baylor coach Grant Teaff went to the NCAA rules committee and told the group that Franklin made a liar out of Teaff's daddy.

"The elder Teaff always said you get the ball back if you hold the other team on its side of the fifty-yard line," Robert Heard wrote in his 1978 feature in *Texas Football* magazine. "But the Bears did that twice in that game and got six points scored against them. The shock turned what should have been a close game into a 24-0 drubbing."

In 1978, the rule was changed that when a field goal is missed, the other team gets possession of the ball at the line of scrimmage instead of the twenty-yard line. So, if Johannson would have missed his sixty-nine-yarder that day under the new rule, East Texas State would have gotten the ball on the ACU forty-eight-yard line instead of the twenty. That's a difference of thirty-two yards in field position.

Later, the two-inch tee that Johansson, Little, Erxleben and Franklin used was outlawed, meaning college kickers had to kick the ball off the ground, the same as the kickers in the National Football League.

Oddly enough, only Franklin had any success in the NFL. Johansson, whose pro career was even shorter than his one season in college, has no regrets, however.

"I've been fortunate," he said. "I enjoyed it so much. To play with such athletes was an unbelievable experience. I got to meet

Roger Staubach. I'm just grateful to get the opportunity. Just to put on an NFL helmet was such an honor."

Ove Johansson with the ball he used to kick his record-breaking field goal. Courtesy of Ove Johansson.

Johansson finished the 1977 season with the Philadelphia Eagles, playing the last five games, and then re-signed with the team in 1978. He drove to Philadelphia for training camp, only to receive a call from Philly coach Dick Vermeil, telling him that he had been claimed by the Dallas Cowboys.

"I got a call then from Gil Brandt (the Cowboys' director of player personnel)," Johansson recalled. "He said 'Get your butt to Thousand Oaks (California).'"

Johansson stayed with the Cowboys through preseason, but the Cowboys released him and signed Rafael Septien, who had been the league's top rookie kicker the season before but had been cut by the Los Angeles Rams."

So Johansson gave up his pro football career and eventually opened his investments business in Amarillo in 1980. But he is still thrilled to claim the title of kicking the world's longest field goal.

"I've had a lot of fun with it over the years," Johansson said of his record. "At age fifty-eight, I still kick every week with the high school kickers in Amarillo and I work with the West Texas A&M kickers."

By the way, wonder what ever happened to April, the pretty girl he saw in the stands that day in Irving that caused him to come to Texas and eventually kick the world's longest field goal?

Well, they have been married thirty years now. Their daughter graduated from Abilene Christian and their son is a student at Pepperdine University.

And that's what love's got to do with it.

A Day that Changed a Life

October 16, 1976, is remembered for more than just long field goals. It is also the fateful day that changed University of Houston head football coach Art Briles' life forever.

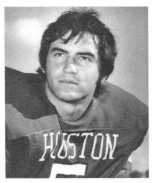

Art Briles as a sophomore receiver at Houston. Courtesy of the University of Houston sports information department.

Years later, Briles admitted he had no premonition of what that day would bring or how it would affect his life. A sophomore wide receiver at UH that fall, he was thinking only about the Cougars' game that day against Southern Methodist University.

It is a seven-hour drive from tiny Rule in West Texas to Houston, so Dennis and Wanda Briles didn't get to see their youngest son play football that often. Of the nine schools in the Southwest Conference, only Texas Christian University's Amon Carter Stadium in Fort Worth and Texas Tech's Jones Stadium in Lubbock were a closer drive from their home in Rule than the Cotton Bowl in Dallas, where SMU played its home games.

As the football calendar turned to October 16, it marked Week Six of a thirteen-week 1976 football season in the Southwest Conference. This was a milestone year in the rich history of the SWC for a number of reasons, although only one or two were apparent that morning.

After having to serve a five-year probationary wait, Houston officially became a member of the Southwest Conference in

1976. It was the first change in years in the makeup of the league, which initially began in 1914. The SWC was unique in that all nine members—except for the University of Arkansas—were located within the borders of the state of Texas. Twenty years later, that would be a factor in the breakup of the SWC and the formation of the Big 12 Conference. In 1976, however, that just meant that many of the league's players had played with and against each other in high school before moving on to the college ranks.

Because of the addition of Houston to the league, the 1976 schedule underwent a major change from the one that SWC fans had become accustomed.

Houston had to open the season with a conference game at Baylor. The Cougars received a less-than-warm welcome to the league in the pregame prayer over the public address system at Baylor Stadium in Waco: "We welcome the University of Houston into our Southwest Conference family. Lord, help us make their visit as memorable as possible."

It was Houston that delivered a message to the rest of the league, however, shocking the Bears 23-5. Just two years earlier, Grant Teaff had led Baylor to the school's first league title in fifty years, the "Miracle on the Brazos" season. The Bears were expected to be one of the leading contenders to win the 1976 crown and a berth in the Cotton Bowl that went to the SWC champion.

The victory was an omen of things to come as 1976 would eventually be remembered as the "Cinderella Season" for the Cougars.

Although Houston lost its second game of the season, falling 49-14 to Florida, the Cougars bounced back with a surprising 21-10 win over Texas A&M the next week. Houston found itself with a 2-0 conference record, having already beaten two of the league's chief title contenders, heading to the October 16 date with SMU in the Cotton Bowl.

1976 was a milestone year in the Southwest Conference for a couple of other reasons, too. Although no one realized it on

October 16, this would be the final season for the league's two most successful coaches. Arkansas and Texas had moved their game to December 4 for television, a primetime telecast to close out the 1976 regular season.

That night, both Darrell Royal at Texas and Frank Broyles at Arkansas announced their retirements from coaching. Both had been on the sidelines for nearly two decades, winning numerous conference titles as well as several national championships.

Royal and Broyles were two of the biggest names in college coaching, and the Southwest Conference would not be the same without the two. But that announcement was still nearly two months away.

On the morning of October 16, 1976, however, Briles was looking forward to the Cougars' game that afternoon with SMU and to seeing his parents after the game.

"They didn't get to see me play that often," Briles recalled. "I talked to my mom the night before the game. I remember during the game looking up in the stands and looking for them, but I was never able to see them. I just thought I wasn't looking in the right place."

What Briles didn't know was that his parents and his aunt Elsie Kittley had been killed that morning in a car wreck on the way to the game. Two oil tankers had reportedly been racing. When a truck driven by twenty-five-year-old Lowry Ero of Jacksboro went around the other truck, it collided head-on with the Briles' car, two-and-a-half miles east of Newcastle on Highway 380. Ero suffered only minor injuries, but Mr. and Mrs. Briles and Kittley were killed instantly.

Dennis Briles, forty-four, had been his son's high school coach, leading the Bobcats to the Class B state title game in 1973. Art was the star quarterback of the team, but Big Sandy beat Rule 25-0 to win its first of three consecutive state championships.

Dennis, honored as the citizen of the year in his hometown of Rule in 1975, had given up his coaching duties to become the principal at Rule High School. Wanda Briles, forty-two, was a special education teacher at Rule. Kittley, sixty-six, was Wanda's older sister, but they were much closer than that. Kittley had raised Wanda since birth after their mother died in childbirth. She was more like Art's grandmother than aunt.

Houston coach Bill Yeoman learned of the fatal accident just moments before the kickoff of the game. He decided to not tell Briles until after the game. Looking back, Briles is not upset that he wasn't informed immediately.

"There is not a proper way to handle it," he said.

As the Cougars celebrated their victory over the Ponies, Yeoman called Briles, linebacker Paul Humphreys who was Briles' closest friend on the team, and assistant coach Larry French who had recruited Briles, into an office just off the Cougars' locker room at the Cotton Bowl.

"When he asked me to come in there, I knew something was wrong," Briles said.

After learning of the accident, Briles and Humphreys flew immediately to Abilene.

Ed Fouts, Dennis' childhood friend who was on the school board that first hired Dennis to coach at Rule, met Briles and Humphreys at the Abilene airport and drove them to Rule.

"He couldn't accept it," Fouts said of Briles' reaction. "He didn't take it as good as Eddie (Briles' older brother). Dennis had quit coaching because he wanted to be able to see Art's games. He had also started farming land that Wanda had inherited."

On the following Monday, classes were cancelled at Rule as nearly everyone in town crowded into the school's gymnasium for the three funerals.

"Dennis did a tremendous job for us," Fouts recalled. "It didn't matter who the kid was, Dennis treated everyone the same. The kids respected him."

Despite a knee injury and the tragic death of his parents, Briles finished the season with the Cougars, who won the SWC championship and earned a return trip to the Cotton Bowl.

"I had knee surgery in the off-season," Briles recalled. "It didn't respond. But, emotionally, I was at ends. I thought a change of scenery might ease my pain. Everywhere I went on campus at Houston, people would say there is the guy whose parents were killed."

Briles gave up football, transferred to Texas Tech, and earned his degree. But it was during his time away from football at Texas Tech that he decided to become a football coach, following in the footsteps of his father.

"It changed me tremendously," Briles said of the death of his parents. "It made me a little more serious, but at the same time more thankful. I could see how precious life is. It made me a little more understanding, which helped in my coaching profession. We're in the kid-helping business. I can have empathy with kids."

Briles became one of the most successful high school coaches in Texas. After stints as an assistant coach at Sundown and Sweetwater, he spent four years as the head coach and athletic director at Hamlin and two years at Georgetown before taking over a downtrodden program at Stephenville. He turned Stephenville into the state's top football program of the 1990s. In his twelve seasons there, the Yellow Jackets won four Class 4A state championships.

His teams were noted for their wide-open offense. In fact, Stephenville's 1998 state championship team set a national record by accumulating 8,650 yards total offense.

Briles left Stephenville to become the running backs coach at Texas Tech. In 2003, he was hired as the first former Cougar player to become the head coach at the University of Houston, returning to the campus that he had left following the 1976 season because the memories were too painful.

His coaching success has continued at Houston as Briles led the Cougars to bowl games in three of his first four seasons on the UH campus, winning the Conference USA title in 2006 and earning a berth against South Carolina in the Liberty Bowl.

"I'm really proud of him," Fouts said of Briles. "He's a great guy."

Despite his enormous success, Briles has never forgotten October 16, 1976, the day that changed his life forever.

A Cruel Twist of Fate

This is the story of Jaxon Brigman, a journeyman professional golfer who now lives in the Dallas suburb of Frisco.

To completely understand the gut-wrenching turn of events
that changed Brigman's career forever, one must first understand
how professional golf works. The PGA Tour is basically a closed fraternity. Golfers must go through an arduous qualifying process to
join that fraternity. Once golfers make it on the Tour, they must finish among the top 125 on the money list each year just to maintain
the privilege of playing with the world's greatest golfers. Otherwise,
it is back to the qualifying tournament at the end of the year.

Life on the PGA Tour, of course, can be very rewarding. The
money is unbelievable, the perks and endorsements are plenti-
ful. It is living life in first class. Thousands of golfers dream of
making it on the PGA Tour, but few ever get the chance. Many
spend years chasing that dream, however, playing on the
Nationwide Tour (the Triple-A minor league version of the PGA
Tour) or the numerous non-PGA-Tour-affiliated mini-tour or
satellite tour events such as the Tight Lies Tour in Texas, New
Mexico, and Louisiana where golfers pay steep entry fees just for
the hopes of winning it back in prize money.

And then, after a year of just trying to make ends meet, paying
as much as an $850 entry fee to play in a tournament no one has
heard of for the right to compete for prize money that will only
pay that week's expenses if they are lucky, golfers will fork over
$5,000 more for the right to compete in the year-end PGA Tour
Qualifying Tournament.

The PGA Tour Qualifying is an endurance test. The first stages are four-day, seventy-two-hole tournaments, often attracting as many as a thousand golfers who share the dream of trying to earn the right to play with Tiger Woods and the other stars of the PGA Tour. In 2006, the PGA actually added a pre-qualifying event, just to get into the first stage. The top finishers in the first-stage tournaments advance to the second stage, also four-day, seventy-two-hole events. Some golfers, depending on how they did the previous year on the PGA or Nationwide Tour, are exempt from either the first or second stages.

The top scores from the second-stage tournaments, as well as those who finished between No. 125 and No. 150 on the PGA Tour money list the previous year, move on to the third and final stage, which is a six-day, 108-hole marathon held in December. The top thirty at the final stage earn exempt playing status on the PGA Tour. The next fifty qualify for the Nationwide Tour. The remaining golfers in the final-stage field of 160 become partially exempt on the Nationwide Tour for the following year, meaning they can get into those tournaments if they aren't full.

All of that expense, time, effort, and stress are invested for the right to play in tournaments in which golfers won't earn a penny if they fail to make the cut that particular week. Yet thousands of professional golfers still pursue that dream each year, hoping they will be the lucky winner of golf's lottery, qualifying for the right to play on the PGA Tour where nearly 100 golfers won more than $1 million in 2006.

Which brings us to the story of Jaxon Brigman, a three-time Class 3A state champion in high school at Abilene Wylie and a standout collegiate golfer at Oklahoma State. Brigman has been to the PGA Tour Qualifying Tournament thirteen times since turning professional in 1994, with varying degrees of success.

His unbelievable twist of fate occurred in 1999. The third stage of the PGA Tour Qualifying Tournament that year was being held at Doral Country Club in Miami, and Brigman fired an impressive 65 on the final day of the event, putting himself into contention for possibly earning an exempt status on the PGA Tour for the first time in his career.

"Going to the last hole, I knew I was close," Brigman recalled. "The last hole for me was No. 9, which is a par three. We had a long wait (before teeing off), and I saw my dad (Jack Brigman, an Abilene accountant who was caddying for his son) talking to a rules official. I assumed he was asking where I stood, but I wasn't going to ask. But I was thinking I needed a birdie on the last hole to qualify."

Brigman said he hit a good shot, a six-iron to within six feet of the hole.

"If I make this, I make it on the Tour," Brigman was thinking to himself as he stood over his putt.

"But I hit it through the break, I hit it too hard," he lamented. "I had a tough downhill putt coming back, but I made it for a par three. I was disappointed because it was a very makeable putt. We shook hands (with his playing partners) and I looked at my parents for their reaction."

His mother and father, however, didn't know, either, whether or not his missed birdie putt would spoil his chance of qualifying for the PGA Tour. Brigman said his mind was still on the missed putt when he went to the scorer's tent to sign and turn in his scorecard.

"I handed it to the guy (tournament official) in the tent and asked, 'Would you add it up?' Brigman recalled. "He said 65 (Brigman agreed, knowing that was the score he had shot)."

Tournament officials posted Brigman's 65 on the scoreboard, and he then took the shuttle back to the scoreboard near the clubhouse to await the tournament's conclusion.

"We had to wait about forty-five minutes to see if we made it," he remembered. "Then The Golf Channel (which was televising the event) announced that I was going to make it. People were coming up to me, congratulating me. I'm hugging my parents and my girlfriend (who is now his wife)."

Brigman said he then saw a rules official drive up in a golf cart and come walking toward him.

"I thought uh-oh," he said.

"Jaxon, what did you make on No. 13?" the official asked.

"A birdie," Brigman replied.

"I'm sorry," the official said. "You have a four on your score-card."

"I hit the floor and started crying," Brigman said. "I thought I was disqualified. I didn't know the rule."

In golf, one's playing partner keeps the other player's score. Brigman's playing partner, former Auburn golfer Jay Hobby, had circled Brigman's score on the par-four 13th hole, correctly signifying that he had made a birdie on the hole. But he had inadvertently written down a "four," rather than the accurate "three" on that hole. Neither Brigman nor the tournament official in the scoring tent whom Brigman had asked to add up the score to double-check his math had caught the mistake.

If Brigman's score had improved his actual total, he would have been disqualified. Since the mistake cost him a stroke, he wasn't disqualified, however. But he did have to take the higher score, meaning he posted a 66 rather than a 65 in his final round.

Unfortunately, the difference between a 65 and 66 meant the difference between being able to call himself a PGA Tour golfer or just another pro golfer who had failed to qualify for the Tour. That 66 meant Brigman has missed qualifying for the PGA Tour by one stroke.

To his credit, Brigman has never ducked questions about that fateful day, always acknowledging the fact that it was his own mistake. He has no one to blame but himself.

Brigman has gone back to the PGA Tour Qualifying each year since 1999, but he has never come as close to qualifying as he did that year. In 2006, in his thirteenth try at the PGA Tour Qualifying event, he failed to make it past the second stage.

He has played in six PGA Tour events in his twelve-year professional career, getting in on a sponsor's exemption or making the field through the Monday qualifier, a one-day event in which more than 100 golfers will try to earn four or fewer spots in that week's tournament.

He has proven he can play with the world's top golfers, placing eleventh at the Texas Open in 2001. Brigman qualified for the Byron Nelson Classic in Irving in 2005, tying for tenth and earning the largest paycheck of his career of $148,000. By comparison, golfers play for a total purse of $100,000 on the Tight Lies Tour, now known as the Adams Golf Pro Golf Tour.

Under PGA Tour rules, a golfer who finishes among the top ten in a tournament is automatically exempt to play the next week. The Colonial in Fort Worth was the following week after the Byron Nelson. Because the Colonial is an invitational, he couldn't play in it, but Brigman went to the St. Jude Classic in Memphis the following week, making the cut and finishing forty-second for his second straight payday on the PGA Tour.

Unfortunately, he has not played in a PGA Tour event since, unable to gain entrance into the closed fraternity. Unlike most journeyman golfers, however, Brigman has actually made money playing golf. He was the leading money winner on the Tight Lies Tour in 2003 and 2004. After playing mostly on the Nationwide Tour, in addition to his two PGA Tour event successes, in 2005, Brigman finished second on the Tight Lies Tour money list in 2006, earning more than $67,000.

"This tour has been a good fall-back for me," Brigman said of the Tight Lies Tour. "I've played well enough to make a profit. That is hard to do because you're not playing for much money."

Meanwhile, Brigman plans to keep trying to complete his dream and hopefully qualify for the PGA Tour.

"What else am I going to do?" he asked. "If I'm making money, why change professions to go into an entry level position. I wake up every morning and still look forward to playing golf. The potential is there for income. If I could make the PGA Tour some day, my income could be a lot."

So the dream lives on, even though Brigman, who now has a young daughter to support, too, still has to answer questions about the day he signed the incorrect scorecard, a mistake that had unbelievable consequences on his career. In a sport that can be difficult, at best, it was golf's cruelest twist of fate.

A "Hall of Famer"

Every university has a sports hall of fame in which it honors outstanding former players, coaches and benefactors. But perhaps there has never been a hall of fame inductee quite like Neel LeMond.

LeMond never played a down of football at McMurry University in Abilene. He never suited up for a McMurry basketball game, either. He was never officially enrolled in a class at the school. And he's not a major benefactor.

But when LeMond was inducted into the McMurry Athletic Hall of Honor in 1996, he was possibly the most popular inductee ever—and the most well known.

For fifty years, Neel, who probably functions at about a twelve-year-old level, has been every bit as much of an institution on the McMurry campus as Radford Auditorium or Indian Stadium, recently renamed Wilford Moore Stadium.

"Neel is in a man's body," said former McMurry quarterback and head football coach Steve Keenum. "But he is a child in mind and spirit."

Neel first arrived at McMurry in 1956 at age eighteen when his father, a Methodist minister, moved into a home on Ross Street across from Indian Stadium.

McMurry immediately became Neel's home. His father died a few years later, but he and his mother continued to live adjacent to the McMurry campus until her death in 1990. He moved to Houston to live with a sister-in-law for several years, but then moved back to Abilene and lives now in a group home not far from the McMurry campus.

In 1995, during the brief time that Neel was living away from the only home he'd ever known, he returned for McMurry's homecoming football game and Keenum had him deliver the pregame speech to the team.

When I arrived in Abilene as the new sports editor in 1986, Neel quickly befriended me and sought me out at each home game to provide me with some "important" tidbit of information I needed to know about the McMurry team.

Neel never missed an Indians' football or basketball practice. He was often on the bench during a game, getting a drink for a player or doing whatever was asked of him. It wasn't unusual to see Neel in the huddle during a timeout.

"When I arrived back on the scene in 1959, we'd always end practice in football by putting Neel in the backfield," said longtime McMurry coach Hershel Kimbrell. "Every player would try to tackle him, but he'd go for a touchdown."

Neel became a part of more than just McMurry athletics. He was part of campus life as well. In 1991, the *Totem*, McMurry's yearbook, was dedicated to Neel. Professors allowed

Neel LeMond at his induction ceremony into the McMurry Hall of Honor. Courtesy of Neel LeMond.

Neel to sit in their classes. He'd take notes and professors often would give him a "grade." Legend says only one ever gave him a "B." The rest were all "A's." Kimbrell said Neel "took" his coaching class every year.

For thirty-four years, until he moved to Houston, every McMurry student knew Neel—and he knew them. Coaches, faculty and students alike looked out for Neel, helped him out and became his friend. In return, they had the most loyal supporter one could ever have.

"Neel was a permanent fixture for so long," Kimbrell said. "We never had a more loyal Indian than Neel LeMond."

"Neel is somebody who is the epitome of a giving spirit," Keenum added. "He loves McMurry more than anyone I know."

Now, more than fifty years after he first arrived on campus, Neel can still be found at every McMurry home football or basketball game. He has given all of his love and trust to McMurry for all of his life, and the school returned the favor by inducting him into its Athletic Hall of Honor in 1996.

In a sports world seemingly filled today with unpleasant stories of drug or spousal abuse, contract disputes and greed, Neel's Hall of Honor induction remains one of my favorite heartwarming stories.

A Texas Treasure

Is there anything more unique to Texas than Dave Campbell's *Texas Football* magazine? For nearly a half century, the Lone Star State's football fans have eagerly awaited the arrival of the magazine each summer to find the "scoop" about the prospects of their favorite college and high school teams and to whet their appetites for the upcoming football season.

From the author's collection.

"I would never have imagined in 1960 that the magazine would become what it is today, forty-seven years later," said Campbell, the publication's founder who is still going strong himself in his 80s.

Although Campbell, who spent nearly forty years as sports editor of the *Waco Tribune-Herald*, sold the publication to conglomerate Host Communications several years ago, he is still involved in its operation. Not only does his name remain on the cover but he also writes a column each year for the magazine, lends his input to editorial decisions, and conducts an annual tour of the state to promote the magazine.

"It has surpassed all my hopes and expectations," Campbell said. "Just think, we actually outlived the old Southwest

Conference, which was in full flower when we started. I could not have dreamed that we would be going when the Southwest Conference was dead, but that's the way it worked out."

What fans may not know, however, is that the demise of minor league baseball actually played a significant role in the creation of *Texas Football* magazine.

"In those days, Waco had a pro baseball team, the Waco Pirates, which were a farm club of the Pittsburgh Pirates," Campbell recalled. "As air conditioning set in and television came along, attendance fell off and Pittsburgh moved that farm club. What had been an easy job for a sports editor, who was writing five columns a week in those days, became a real labor of some problem to find appropriate subjects to columnize on day by day.

"So I would really hawk the newsstands in mid-summer awaiting those football annuals to make their appearance so I could pick up some idea how they thought the Southwest Conference would do. There was no high school coverage at all."

In the summer of 1959 Campbell conceived the idea of producing his own magazine.

"When the summer annuals came out that year, they were strictly focused on college football," he said. "The pros had not reached nearly the level that they have now. Those college publications covered the waterfront as far as the national scene was concerned. There was absolutely no coverage of high school football in any part of the country.

"That year as I hurriedly and anxiously looked through the Southwest Conference section, I was just struck by the number of typographical errors there were in the coverage and also the errors of fact. I was closely following Southwest Conference football myself, and I just thought there were all sorts of errors and a misleading picture of upcoming events. So it occurred to me that as passionate as Texas people are about their football and as anxiously as they await the upcoming season, surely something better than this could be done."

Campbell said that was the "seeds from which *Texas Football* sprang."

"I started checking what it would cost to produce a regional publication that would give high school coverage and extensive Southwest Conference coverage," he recalled. "In those days, we were giving five or six pages to each Southwest Conference school, while those other publications were giving only an extended paragraph or two.

"We were flying blind. I was sports editor (in Waco). Three or four guys on my staff were helping me. We were all newspaper people, not magazine people. We sent out questionnaires to high school coaches, and we made personal trips to each of the Southwest Conference campuses. We talked to the coaches and some of the star players to get in-depth coverage. We put together a ninety-six-page publication with color only on the cover. We went to press and put it on the newsstands in early July that year."

Campbell said he and his staff then sat back to await the results.

"It was really hailed," he recalled. "It was given a grand reception by the sports writers around the state. The reception was just terrific from the readers, and all we did was LOSE $5,000. The next year I was so encouraged I kept on and lost only $3,000. The next year my wife said we're not going to keep doing this, but we did it the third year and we started getting close to the break-even point. Fortunately, we kept doing it and we crossed the profit line. Here we are forty-seven years later with a much larger publication and color throughout, with great stories and more extensive coverage. I'm very proud of the product."

From University of Texas wide receiver Jack Collins, who appeared on the first 1960 cover, to former Longhorn running back Earl Campbell and four high school quarterbacks who appeared on the front page of the 2006 issue, it has become a coveted badge of honor to appear on the magazine's cover.

"*Sports Illustrated* supposedly has the jinx about appearing on its cover, but we've had a lot of luck with our covers," Campbell said. "In 1963 we had Darrell Royal and lineman Scott Appleton of Texas on the cover. The Longhorns won the national championship and Appleton was the most heralded lineman in the country. In 1964, (Baylor receiver) Lawrence Elkins appeared on the cover and he became a two-time all-American. Donnie Anderson of Texas Tech was on the cover in 1965. He didn't win a championship, but the Green Bay Packers gave him $711,000 that spring, which was an unheard of sum at that time."

Midland Lee running back Cedric Benson was the first high school player to dominate the cover in 2001. That fall, he led the Rebels to a third consecutive state championship and became the leading rusher in Class 5A history.

"We don't think we have a jinx with our cover," Campbell said.

When asked to offer a favorite story from forty-seven years of publishing the magazine, Campbell laughingly remembers an unusual phone call he received.

"The time the magazine comes off the press is always eagerly awaited, not only by us but by the fans themselves," he said. "One year the magazine was just about to come off the press when we got a phone call from someone in Dallas. I don't have the faintest idea now what his name was, but the man identified himself and said he really, really needed a copy of the magazine."

Campbell said the man was about to leave for Canada and he wanted to know if he could get an early copy of it.

"We told him the magazine wasn't quite to that stage yet, but we told him we'd be happy to get him a copy as soon as we could," Campbell said. "He explained that he was about to get married, and he was going to Canada on his honeymoon."

"I'm going to send you extra money," the voice on the other end of the phone told Campbell. "As soon as you get a copy, if you would air-mail me and send special delivery a magazine to this address in Canada, I would really appreciate it because I've got to have something to do up there on my honeymoon."

Football fans of all types in Texas still eagerly await the arrival *Dave Campbell's Texas Football* magazine each summer.

From Johnny Lam Jones to Jonathan Johnson

The University Interscholastic League state track meet, held in Austin every year, is the largest track meet in the nation. Actually, it is ten track meets rolled into two days, featuring boys and girls competition in five different classifications.

James Griffith believes it is one of the great sporting events held in Texas each year. He should know. The Abilene real estate agent has attended 34 of the last 35 state meets.

"The only one I've missed was the weekend my daughter graduated from Texas A&M," he noted.

The meet used to draw as many as 30,000 fans when it was held in Memorial Stadium. Now, that it has moved to Mike Myers Stadium, the new high-tech track facility at the Univer-

Texas Tech's Jonathan Johnson gives a "guns up" after winning the 800 meter race at the 2004 U.S. Olympic Trials. From the author's collection.

sity of Texas, 15,000 to 20,000 still cram into the stands to watch each year.

So why does Griffith, and thousands of other fans, keep going back to the state high school meet each year?

"I love it," Griffith said. "To me, it is such a wholesome competition. You always see things you never expect, things you don't normally see. You see kids do things you think isn't possible. It is an individual and a team competition. There are eight winners in every race. There is a winner in every lane."

Maybe that is one thing that makes the state meet in Texas such an interesting, unique competition. There are no preliminary races. Every event is a final, featuring eight participants. Athletes have to place in the top two at their district meet to qualify for regional. Only the top two from each of four regional meets around the state advance to the state meet. So it is, indeed, the best of the best who eventually end up competing for a gold medal in Austin.

Many of the nation's legendary track and field athletes have competed in Texas on their way to stardom: Babe Didrikson Zaharias of Beaumont; Texas Woman's University high jumper Louise Ritter; San Benito sprinter Bobby Morrow; decathlete Rafer Johnson of Hillsboro; University of Houston sprinter/long jumper Carl Lewis; and shot putter Randy Matson of Pampa are just some of the nearly 100 Olympic gold medalist either born in Texas or who lived in the state at the time of their competition.

One of the state's youngest gold medalists was Johnny "Lam" Jones of Lampasas, who qualified for the 1976 Olympics in Montreal and was a member of the U.S. gold-medal winning 4x100 relay team just months after he electrified the crowd and set several records at the UIL state meet in Austin.

Today, more than thirty years after Johnny Lam's performance, long-time track fans still talk about his incredible come-from-behind victory on the anchor leg of the mile relay as the greatest performance in state track meet history.

"He was seventy-five yards behind when he got the baton," Griffith recalled. "It was unreal. It is the biggest thrill I've had watching the state meet."

Jones went on to play football for the Texas Longhorns and New York Jets in addition to winning an Olympic gold medal.

Griffith also lists two other mile relays among his all-time favorite moments at the state meet. Dallas Lincoln's relay team of Joe and Gene Pouncy, Rufus Shaw, and John Dilley outdueled Austin Anderson's relay team, which came into the race with the top time in the nation, to win the gold medal. And Art Briles, now the head football coach at the University of Houston, anchored Rule to the mile-relay victory over Big Sandy in a driving rainstorm that clinched the Class B state team title for the Bobcats in 1974.

One other event that Griffith remembers fondly is also my own personal favorite in fifteen years of covering the state meet as a sports writer. That was the performance of Abilene High's Jonathan Johnson in 2001.

At the Class 5A state meet that year, Johnson shattered the state's longest standing record. With the crowd roaring as he pulled away down the backstretch, Johnson ran a 1:48.21 to win the 800, eclipsing the old mark of 1:49.20 that had stood for thirty-four years. His time was the seventh fastest 800 ever run in the United States by a high school halfmiler.

"I knew I had a shot at the record," Johnson said after the race. "I'd been working at running the first lap at 52.5 or 53.0. On the back side (of the second lap), I just took off. I just pushed myself. I didn't hear my split. I was just focused on the race."

"Jonathan hadn't been pushed all year," said Randy Martin, his coach at Abilene High, "so I knew it was just a matter of time and he would get the record. Conditions were perfect, and the fans really helped him as he came down the straightaway."

That performance alone would have been enough to make Johnson's effort the top achievement of the 2001 meet. But in the final race of the night—and Abilene High needing at least a second place in the 1,600-meter relay to claim the Class 5A boys' team title—Johnson outdid his own performance of slightly more than an hour earlier, rekindling the memories of Johnny Lam's anchor leg of the mile relay twenty-five years earlier.

The Eagles were in third place when Johnson received the baton for the final leg of the relay from teammate Robert Spells. Johnson was nearly twenty meters behind Houston Washington's anchor man James Bell.

"I wasn't for sure," Johnson replied later, when asked if he thought he could make up that much of a difference. "I told myself that we'd made it this far, I was going to do whatever it took to get first."

Johnson caught Bell on the final curve, and the two headed down the homestretch at Mike Myers Stadium stride for stride. Johnson leaned at the tape to edge Bell. Abilene's relay team of Tyree Gailes, Shawon Harris, Spells and Johnson was clocked in 3:11.69, and Houston Washington was right behind at 3:11.72. Johnson was timed in 45.8 for his split on the final leg of the relay.

"This is the greatest day of my career," said Johnson at the time, managing a big smile on his tired face. "I wanted the record, and the mile relay wanted to win. It was a great day."

Johnson, however, had even more great moments awaiting him on the track. By the time his four-year career at Texas Tech had ended in 2005, Johnson had earned sixteen all-Big 12 honors and won three consecutive Big 12 titles in the 800 meters. He also helped lead Tech to the school's first conference track and field championship. Johnson captured nine all-America honors during his collegiate career, won two NCAA titles in the 800, and posted a personal best of 1:44.77 in the 800, the third best time ever recorded by a collegian.

Like Jones, Johnson became an Olympian. Running in an event normally dominated by veteran athletes in the late 20s or 30s, Johnson, a college junior at the time, won the 800 at the 2004 U.S. Olympic Trials, crossing the finish line while giving the Texas Tech "Guns Up" sign.

"He was so tight right before the race," Texas Tech track coach Wes Kittley recalled. "I told him I'll see you at the finish line and you give them the guns up when you win. He kind of smiled and it kind of broke the edge with him. After the race, I asked him how in the world did you remember to do that?"

"Coach, it was the last thing you told me," Johnson replied with a laugh.

Johnson advanced through the first two rounds of the 800 meters at the 2004 Olympics in Athens, Greece, before he suffered dehydration and failed to win a medal in the finals.

But, like fellow Olympian Johnny "Lam" Jones of Lampasas, the track and field world "discovered" Abilene's Jonathan Johnson for the first time at the 2001 state high school meet in Austin.

As Griffith said of the UIL state meet: "You see things you don't normally see."

Baseball's Greatest
Home Run Hitter

U ntil Barry Bonds of the San Francisco Giants came along, the professional single-season home run record belonged to a long-forgotten slugger from an equally forgotten minor league in Texas.

When Bonds set the major league record with seventy-three home runs in 2001, all baseball fans knew he snapped the previous standard of seventy homers that had been set by St. Louis Cardinals slugger Mark McGwire just three years earlier.

Of course, the exciting McGwire-Sammy Sosa duel for the home run record in 1998 is credited with revitalizing baseball, reminding fans of the epic 1961 battle between New York Yankee teammates Roger Maris and Mickey Mantle when Maris broke Babe Ruth's record by hitting sixty-one home runs.

Long forgotten in the home run discussion, however, is Joe Baumann, the greatest minor league slugger in baseball history. Baumann, playing in the Class C Longhorn League in 1954 in the dusty outback of eastern New Mexico and far West Texas, far from the media scrutiny that Maris, Mantle, McGwire, Sosa and Bonds faced, had a season that was unparalleled.

Playing for the Artesia (New Mexico) Drillers in 1952 and 1953, Baumann posted back-to-back seasons with fifty-plus home runs and a .370 batting average. Those seasons were just a warm-up for his record-setting 1954 campaign.

Baumann, a career minor leaguer, joined the Roswell (New Mexico) Rockets in 1954. He hit seventy-two home runs, a professional record that stood until Bonds topped his mark in 2001. He batted .406 that season, collected 190 hits and drove in 224 runs, leading the league in six offensive categories.

On September 1, 1954, Baumann, who was thirty-two during his record-setting season, set a Longhorn League record with four home runs and nine RBIs in a 15-8 win over Sweetwater. The next day, he hit home run number sixty-nine of the season off Midland left-hander Ralph Atkinson at a home game in Roswell. That tied the minor league record, set by Bob Crues of the Amarillo Gold Sox in 1948 and Joe Hauser of Minneapolis in 1933.

It took another week before Baumann finally got the record. His seventieth homer came in Artesia in the first game of a doubleheader off Jose Gallardo. With the burden finally lifted, Baumann hit two more homers in the nightcap to finish with seventy-two.

Lest you think the ballparks were small and the pitching was woefully weak in the Longhorn League in 1954—both of which were probably true—consider this: The runner-up to Baumann in the league home run race hit only forty-three that year, twenty-nine fewer than Baumann.

Baumann continued to live in Roswell, New Mexico, in relative obscurity until his death in 2005 at age eighty-three.

Bobby and Mickey

The Ballpark in Arlington played host to the Major League Baseball's All-Star Game in 1995. It was the day before the All-Star Game, however, when the phone rang at 5 A.M. at Bobby Richardson's home in South Carolina.

Richardson's long-time friend Mickey Mantle was on the other end of the line.

"I want you to pray for me," Mantle told Richardson. "I'm really hurting."

Richardson, who was already planning to fly to Texas for the All-Star Game, visited Mantle in the hospital the next day.

"I walked into the hospital room and he said, 'I can't wait to tell you I'm a Christian. I've accepted Jesus Christ as my Savior,'" Richardson recalled. "He had a real peace those last few days."

Richardson and Mantle, teammates for twelve years on some of the greatest New York Yankee teams of all time, were close friends, even though two personalities couldn't have been more different. Richardson, a deeply religious man whose two sons are both Methodist ministers, often led team devotions when he played for the Yankees. Mantle, who lived in Dallas after his retirement from baseball, was a heavy drinker and was often out all night partying.

Richardson said he had witnessed to Mantle for years. When another teammate, Roger Maris, died of cancer, Richardson delivered the eulogy at his funeral.

"Mickey was there and he came up to me, crying," Richardson said. "Roger had been the picture of health at age fifty-one and

Mickey had been drinking. He told me 'I want you to speak at my funeral.' I thought he was joking."

He wasn't. A couple of weeks after the All-Star Game, Richardson received another call, this time from Roy True, Mantle's lawyer, to come to Dallas because Mantle had taken a turn for the worse. In Mantle's final days, only Richardson and his wife and Mantle's family were allowed in the hospital room to see the former slugger.

Mantle's funeral at Lovers Lane United Methodist Church in Dallas was nationally televised by ESPN, and Richardson said he was overwhelmed by the response he received after conducting the funeral.

"I received 400 to 500 letters," he said. "I got probably 100 letters from people who had named their sons Mickey after Mantle. When the media found out I was in Dallas, all three networks wanted to send trucks out to the house where I was staying to talk about Mickey's final days. It was amazing."

Richardson is retired now and still lives in his native South Carolina.

He signed with New York at age seventeen out of high school in Sumter, South Carolina, and made the Yankees at age nineteen. Richardson had a .266 batting average during his career from 1955-1966 with the Yankees, although he hit better than .300 twice. In 1962 he batted .301, led the American League with 209 hits, and finished runner-up to Mantle in the voting for the American League MVP Award.

The 1961 Yankees set a record with 225 home runs that season, a mark that held for more than thirty-five years. Richardson laughingly points out he contributed three of those home runs.

He was the head baseball coach at the University of South Carolina from 1970-1976. In 1975, his Gamecocks were 51-4 going into the final two games of the season but lost twice to Cliff Gustafson's Texas Longhorns in the College World Series finals.

Richardson quit coaching to make a run for Congress as a conservative Republican.

"I had no political ambitions," he said. "But Gerald Ford and I were friends and he asked me to run. I lost by 1,500 votes out of 28,000."

It was during that political race that Richardson said he experienced the greatest thrill of his baseball career.

"My first check for my campaign was $500 from Gene Autry (the former owner of the Los Angeles Angels)," he said. "I went out to Anaheim for an old-timers game, and Mantle and Joe DiMaggio said they would fly anywhere and do anything to help me get elected."

On an October night in 1976—the same night Chris Chambliss hit a game-winning home run for the Yankees in the World Series and less than a month before the election—DiMaggio came to Richardson's hometown. A crowd of 5,000 attended the dinner, and DiMaggio signed autographs for everyone there.

"Imagine how much that's worth now," Richardson said. "I still have people coming up to me in my hometown with DiMaggio-autographed baseballs."

After his ill-fated political run, Richardson served as athletic director and baseball coach at Liberty College until his retirement in 1990.

Richardson had a terrific baseball career, but a generation of fans may best remember him for a nationally televised eulogy delivered at Mickey Mantle's funeral on a summer afternoon in Texas.

The Night the Lights Went Out

In thirty-plus seasons of covering high school and college football games, I think I've seen just about everything.

I've covered a game in which snow covered the field to a point that one couldn't see the yard lines. There was the night in which the fog was so thick that an extra-point kick just disappeared as it went through the uprights. Or the night the north wind was so strong that it blew an extra-point kick that had had already cleared the crossbar back into the end zone.

Five inches of rain during a game made for another interesting night. A bucket placed under a hole in the pressbox roof was required to catch the water. The rain was so heavy that the bucket had to be dumped twice each quarter. By the second half, mud-covered uniforms made it impossible to read numbers on the backs of jerseys.

I've also sat through long delays because of lightning, tornado warnings, and power outages. I've even had one game canceled because of lightning.

But a Texas Class 5A football game between Abilene High and Odessa High on October 17, 1997, may have been the most bizarre in which I've ever been involved.

There was still plenty of daylight when two teams took the field at Abilene's Shotwell Stadium for pregame warmups. But as time for the 7:30 P.M. kickoff neared, it became obvious that there was a problem. Only every other bank of lights would come on.

Former Abilene Independent School District athletic director Robert Starr said later that a short in the wiring somewhere underground was the culprit. The officials and coaches decided to wait until kickoff time to make a decision. With Starr, Abilene High coach Steve Warren, Odessa High coach Randy Quisenberry, and the game officials meeting on the turf, it was decided that too many areas on the field were too dark to safely play the game.

So what to do? As a crowd of nearly 10,000 watched the meetings take place on the field, the officials and coaches had to decide whether to postpone the game a day or move to another location.

Since Odessa is a three-hour drive from Abilene, Quisenberry obviously didn't want his Bronchos to drive back to Odessa, only to have to turn around and drive back the next morning. The team had made no prior arrangements to spend the night.

Officials decided to move the game across town to McMurry University's Indian Stadium, an on-campus facility that seats only 2,500. When the announcement was made over the public address system at Shotwell Stadium that the game was moving to Indian Stadium, the mad dash for the parking lot and trek across Abilene began.

It was an unbelievable experience to see 10,000 fans move from one stadium to another. Normally a drive of only about five to ten minutes, it took me forty-five minutes to make the short drive. Ron Holmes, the basketball coach at McMurry who was also serving as the school's athletic director at that time, said the cars coming down Sayles Boulevard toward the McMurry campus looked like the final scene from "Field of Dreams." Fans had to park on side streets in the neighborhood, some as far as six blocks or more away from the McMurry campus.

With the two bands standing behind each end zone, fans standing on the track circling the field and the lucky fans who actually had a seat jammed into the bleachers (no reserved seating for this change of venue), the two teams finally kicked off at 9:15 P.M., nearly two hours after the scheduled starting time.

When I got back to my pickup truck after the game, I discovered I had left my lights on. I had a dead battery and had to get someone to give me a jump before I could return to the office to file my story, more than an hour after the newspaper's scheduled final deadline.

And to think, I still had a better night than Abilene High's Coach Warren. Odessa High upset the Eagles 21-14 that night as Abilene lost five fumbles, threw one interception, missed two field goals, and had a touchdown called back because of a penalty.

When Starr finally arrived home after midnight, he received a call to do an interview for Fox Sports Southwest's "High School Sports Extra" about "the night the lights went out in Abilene." It was the final exclamation point on a wild and wacky night.

"No, never in my life," was Starr's response when asked if the veteran coach and athletic director had ever experienced anything quite like that Friday night.

Neither had thousands of other loyal high school football fans who may have been part of the largest, most unexpected traffic jam in Abilene history.

Wylie's Coach for All Seasons

The past president of the 17,000-member Texas High School Coaches Association has only one thing missing from his resume: A second job.

In a profession in which many lead a nomadic existence, moving from job to job every few years, Abilene Wylie head football coach and athletic director Hugh Sandifer's career is in sharp contrast to most in the organization he headed up during the 2005-2006 school year. In fact, Sandifer has had only one employer since he began his coaching career twenty-eight years ago.

In the summer of 1979, Sandifer wrote a letter to his future wife Brenda, who was spending the summer in France, completing her degree in French from Abilene Christian University.

When the two had gotten engaged earlier, Sandifer had told Brenda that he wasn't going to coach. But while Brenda was studying overseas, he was forced to write her a letter, explaining that he had accepted a teaching and coaching job at Wylie, at the time a country school just south of Abilene.

"I wrote her a letter and described where Wylie was, on the road to Buffalo Gap," Sandifer recalled. "But I said, 'Don't worry. I'll only be there a year and then I'll get a real job.'"

Well, twenty-eight years later Sandifer is still at Wylie. So is his wife Brenda, a guidance counselor at the high school. That "real" job will have to wait because Sandifer's name has become synonymous with Wylie's successful athletic program. He has coached just about every sport imaginable, including a remarkable nine-year stint in which he served as the head coach in both football and boys' basketball.

Now in his twenty-second season as the head football coach and athletic director, he has built the Bulldogs' athletic program into one of the most successful Class 3A programs in the state. In fact, Wylie High School received the prestigious Lone Star Cup as the state's top Class 3A athletic and extracurricular program in 2005-2006, the same year Sandifer served as president of the nation's largest coaches' organization. Wylie reached the state tournament in baseball and girls' basketball that year, advanced to the regional tournament final in boys' basketball, reached the state quarterfinals in football just one year after capturing a state championship and won the girls' singles and doubles titles at the Class 3A state tennis tournament.

Hugh Sandifer, long-time coach at Wylie High School. Courtesy of Tim Nelson/AbileneSportz.com.

It marked the second time that Wylie has claimed the Lone Star Cup in five years. The school owns Class 3A state championships in football, girls' basketball, tennis, golf, and track during Sandifer's tenure at Wylie.

He posted a 231-132 record during thirteen seasons as the Bulldogs' boys' basketball coach, winning six district titles. His Wylie football teams had a record of 172-72-4 in his first twenty-one seasons as head coach. They had won ten district crowns, including their eighth in a row in 2006. They had made the play-offs in twelve of the last thirteen seasons. The Bulldogs won a state championship in 2004 and also reached the state title game in 2000. In fact, Wylie has failed to advance to at least the state quarterfinals only once since 2000.

That is 403 wins as a head varsity coach of either basketball or football at Wylie. Not bad for a guy who almost didn't go into coaching.

Integrating Baseball

A tribute to Jackie Robinson can be found today in every major league baseball stadium in America.

Baseball officially retired his number in 1997, fifty years after Robinson became the first African-American to play in the major leagues. The color barrier was finally broken in the sport when Robinson took the field at second base for the Brooklyn Dodgers on April 15, 1947.

A story forgotten with time, however, is the role that a Texas native played in that event. I first learned of Dr. Dan Dodson and the part he played in integrating baseball from the late Howard Green, an interesting, colorful figure in his own right who played a significant role himself in Texas' baseball history.

Dodson grew up in Mount Vernon in East Texas, graduated from McMurry College in Abilene in 1931, got his master's degree at Southern Methodist University in 1935 before going to New York University for his doctorate. He earned his doctorate in 1941 and was launched on a career that would help shape the nation's destiny in civil rights.

When the Harlem riots broke out in 1944, New York City mayor Fiorello LaGuardia established his Committee on Unity to work for racial equality. Dodson was hired as the committee's executive director.

"I was white, Protestant and available," Dodson recalled in a 1977 interview with former *Abilene Reporter-News* editor Ed Wishcamper. "We were presumably fighting a war to end racial discrimination, while our black soldiers were being beaten in the South."

As executive director of the LaGuardia committee, Dodson wrote a letter to both Brooklyn Dodgers' president Branch Rickey and Larry McPhail, president of the New York Yankees, in 1945, asking if he could talk with each about the possibility of integrating baseball.

McPhail shot back a quick but angry letter railing against the "damn professional do-gooders who were not interested in baseball," and said the blacks weren't either. "Neither are you," McPhail retorted. "You and they just want to make trouble."

Rickey's return letter to Dodson was much different, however.

"I think the time has come we can do something about it," Rickey wrote Dodson. Rickey said he had picked "the person we can rely on to break the color line, maybe not the best player, but the best to do this job."

That person, of course, was Jackie Robinson.

Rickey told Dodson if he attempted to break the color line, Dodson would have "to get the pressure groups off my neck."

With LaGuardia's approval, Dodson went to the groups who were protesting baseball's color barrier with his plea. "If you call your efforts off for the rest of this year, I will join you in picketing next year if it doesn't work," he told them.

Robinson, who had played football and baseball at the University of Southern California, was first signed by Rickey in August 1945, spent the 1946 season with Montreal, the Dodgers' AAA team. Robinson led the International League in hitting in 1946, joined the Dodgers in 1947 and became the National League's Rookie of the Year.

Robinson courageously endured the well-chronicled racial insults that followed him in the 1947 season, and thus laid the groundwork for thousands of minority athletes who followed him in all sports.

"It is hard to assess," Dodson responded in that 1977 interview when asked how much of a landmark case the Robinson incident was. "It didn't bring the millennium, but it made a substantial contribution. It was looked to as a model for a lot of other things beyond that."

Howard Green, who died in 2005 in Fort Worth at age 85, became involved in politics as Tarrant County judge and a state legislator. But his most lasting legacy may have been in baseball. After serving his country in World War II, Green, a McMurry graduate like Dodson, left a job as a sports writer with the *Abilene Reporter-News* to become part-owner and general manager of the Abilene Blue Sox, a Dodgers' minor league team, in 1946.

Although Rickey visited Abilene twice during his tenure as president of the Dodgers, Green's most vivid memory of Rickey was an invitation to be his guest at the New York Baseball Writers dinner at the Waldorf-Astoria in early 1947 when Green was still serving as general manager of the Blue Sox in the West Texas-New Mexico League.

Green, who was also founder and president of the Hall-Ruggles chapter of the Society for American Baseball Research, wrote his recollection of Rickey's comments on Robinson during the 1947 meeting fifty years later in a national SABR publication.

"Of course, signing Robinson, breaking the so-called color line, was the right, the moral thing to do," Rickey told the group. "For more than forty years I have waited impatiently for just the right moment to correct an injustice that makes a mockery of our Bill of Rights.

"Baseball was on shaky legal ground. Blacks had died with whites in that terrible conflict (World War II). It would be only a matter of time, I reasoned, before the courts of the land would by decree force our national game into doing the right, the proper, the decent thing. I seized that moment and predicted that the Brooklyn club in the forefront of a just cause will be the dominant club in the National League for the next ten years at least."

History, of course, proved Rickey right.

Green, who became the youngest president in baseball history when he founded the Longhorn League and later the Gulf Coast League in Texas, said Lamesa of the West Texas-New Mexico League was the first club to integrate in Texas. Manager Jay Haney signed shortstop J.W. Wingate in 1951, but

Wingate struggled at both the plate and defensively and didn't finish the season.

In 1952, however, the Dallas Eagles of the Texas League signed pitcher Dave Hoskins, who went 22-10 and won a promotion to the parent Cleveland Indians. The Greenwood, Mississippi, native compiled a 9-4 record in one-plus seasons with the American League team.

Green was inducted into the Texas Baseball Hall of Fame in 1986. As Tarrant County judge from 1968-1976, he also played a key role in the passage of a bond for Turnpike Stadium, which became the eventual home of the Texas Rangers.

Green said Rickey never mentioned integrating the Blue Sox.

"During his visits to Abilene, and in my other contacts, Mr. Rickey never mentioned the possibility of sending an African-American to Abilene," Green recalled. "He was realistic enough to know the precedents had to be broken at other points on the baseball compass. He signed Robinson in August 1945 to a Montreal contract and shortly afterward Roy Campanella and Don Newcombe to the Brooklyn farm club in Nashua, New Hampshire."

But, thanks to Green, the story of Dodson, an unassuming college professor from Texas who played a key, behind-the-scenes role in the integration of baseball, hasn't been forgotten.

Friday Night Lights

The term "Friday Night Lights" has become an integral part of the sports vernacular in the United States, spawning a best-selling book, a successful movie, and a television show all by the same name.

But what does "Friday Night Lights" actually mean? Is the term a positive one, referring to the importance and significant impact that high school football has on life in Texas? Or is it a negative reference, pointing out all that is wrong when too much emphasis is placed on football?

"I don't know," replied Gary Gaines, the athletic director for the Lubbock Independent School District "I never really thought about that in those terms. I've talked to a lot of people from other parts of the country that have called, and they are amazed about the importance football holds out here. But it is just a way of life for us. I don't know how to answer that."

Gaines, of course, was the central figure in H.G. "Buzz" Bissinger's book *Friday Night Lights*. He was the head coach at Odessa Permian High School in 1988 when Bissinger was granted full access to spend a year in Odessa with the Panthers' football team. His book, chronicling that 1988 season, sparked great controversy, especially in Odessa. In fact, a book signing with Bissinger was canceled in Odessa because of concerns for his safety.

It may surprise readers to learn that Gaines has never read the book—and has no plans to read it. He did go see the movie several months after it came out. He said he has never seen the TV show.

So how did Bissinger, a writer from Philadelphia, end up in Odessa, Texas, penning a book that drew both critical acclaim and strong criticism?

"My phone rang one day (in the spring of 1988), and it was Bissinger," Gaines recalled. "He said he wanted to come down here and write a book about how football binds a community together. He said it would be similar to *Hoosiers*. I had just read the book about Bob Knight (John Feinstein's *Season on the Brink*), and I told him I wasn't interested. I told him there had been enough negative written."

Two weeks later, however, Bissinger showed up at Gaines' office.

"He met with the superintendent and the athletic director at the time (John Wilkins, who was also a former successful Permian coach)," Gaines continued. "Basically, he sold us on the fact that he was going to write a positive book about Permian football. He came back in July and stayed a whole year (in Odessa). We gave him free access to everything. He attended practice and sat in coaching staff meetings."

Permian, one of the storied football programs in Texas high school gridiron history with six state championships to its credit, lost 14-9 to Dallas Carter in the Class 5A state semifinals to end the 1988 season.

Bissinger then left Odessa after the football season concluded, and Gaines said he didn't see the author again until the 1989 state championship game. The Mojo, as the Panthers are known to their loyal following, concluded a perfect 16-0 season in 1989 with a 28-14 victory over Houston Aldine in the Class 5A title game, capturing both a state championship and *USA Today's* mythical national high school championship.

The following February, Gaines left Odessa to become an assistant coach at Texas Tech, although his wife Sharon and their two children stayed behind so their son could finish his senior year at Permian.

"The next time I heard from him was in either June or July (1990)," Gaines said. "Buzz called and said 'I've mailed a book to you at your address in Odessa.' He said 'I think you're going to like it.'"

A few days later, Gaines said Sharon called him in Lubbock.

"She was hysterical about how bad the book was," he said. "She was torn up about the racial things in the book."

Lloyd Hill, a black wide receiver who was one of the star players on the 1988 and 1989 Permian teams, was then playing football at Texas Tech, so Gaines called Hill at his dorm and asked him to come over to his office.

"Did you ever hear me or any player or coach ever use the 'N' word?" Gaines asked Hill.

"No, Coach, we wouldn't have played if you talked like that," Hill responded.

"I felt a little better after that," Gaines said. "I've often wondered if his first version of the book wasn't spicy enough, so his publisher had him re-write it. He told me once he had enough material for two books, one on the football team and one on the oil economy in West Texas. But that is why I've never read the book. I know everything that is in it. He missed such a great opportunity to tell the story about a group of kids who sacrificed so much. Of course, the team was so much bigger than the coach and the five kids who were portrayed in the book."

Long-time *Odessa American* columnist Ken Brodnax addressed the racism issue in a retrospective column he wrote in 1998: "…What's more, the author happened upon a situation on the Panther team that was unfortunate," Brodnax wrote. "The focus of the book became Booby Miles, a star running back who got shoved into the background when he suffered an injury. Bissinger seized up Miles as a victim of racism. But he didn't have the historical perspective to understand that the Permian team was trained to operate as an army. If one soldier goes down, others are expected to step in place. And the injured troop takes a spot in the support ranks. It's happened hundreds of times through the years, but the forgotten man had never become the focus of a book. And Miles sulked instead of joining the support forces."

Gaines, who later coached at Abilene High, San Angelo Central and Abilene Christian University before returning to Odessa in 2005 to become the athletic director for the Ector County I.S.D. before taking the Lubbock I.S.D. job in 2007, saw the movie over the Thanksgiving weekend in 2004, several months after it came out.

"I was relieved," he replied, when asked for his reaction to the film. "I was so uptight going in. It could have been a whole lot worse. There is a lot of Hollywood in it, and the factual errors drove people crazy out here. But it was entertaining. I'm glad it didn't portray coaches as buffoons."

Although Gaines said he was never consulted on the movie, he said actor Billy Bob Thornton, who played Gaines in the movie, called him after the filming was completed.

"We talked for about thirty minutes," Gaines said. "We had a great conversation and he was very classy."

The *Odessa American* published a series of articles in October 1998 entitled "Ten Years Later," looking back on what had happened in the ten years since Bissinger's book had put Odessa in what most in that city considered an unfavorable spotlight.

Brodnax concluded his column by writing: "This is not to say that *Friday Night Lights* is a reason for nostalgia. Nor is it to say that it somehow placed a shadow on the community that never will vanish. The book was a bit like medicine. Perhaps it was a bit bitter to the taste, and it probably had some bad side effects that were hard to shake. But the dose also healed a few ills.

"In short, *Friday Night Lights* caused at least some Odessans to look inward and decide to explore ways to correct some of the impressions, whether they were false or merely a result of not being familiar with the local landscape. The true impact, of course, is measured by the fact that people are still talking about the book ten years after the fact."

Now, it has been almost twenty years, and a movie and television show have since followed the book. And Gaines still answers questions about that season, still amazed that people still want to talk about it.

But Gaines hasn't and won't read the book that sparked the controversy, knowing in his own mind that it incorrectly and unfairly stamped a charge of racism on his football team. For that, he feels betrayed by Bissinger, whom Gaines granted full access to his Permian team in 1988.

"Friday Night Lights," however, lives on, whether right or wrong, positively or negatively, as a term describing high school football in Texas.

Guns Up in Miami

Once, they were Red Raiders. Then, they were Dolphins. But forever they will be remembered for what they accomplished against the Aggies.

Zach Thomas, Sammy Morris and Wes Welker—teammates in the 2005 and 2006 seasons with the Miami Dolphins—have more in common than just being teammates on the same National Football League team. They also share the distinction of enjoying one of the most memorable plays in their outstanding collegiate careers at Texas Tech in important victories over Texas A&M. All three remember not only their own personal magical moment against the Aggies but also the key plays by the other two.

"Coach (Mike Leach) would show film of Zach and Sammy making touchdowns during the week of the A&M game," Welker recalled.

"Yeah, we all talk about it," Morris added. "I was on the sideline as a redshirt when Zach intercepted the pass to beat the Aggies. And then when Wes had his punt return, the paper ran a picture of his punt return and my touchdown with the caption 'Déjà vu.' They were almost identical pictures. We were both running for the end zone, and the Corps was in the background, looking disgusted."

"We didn't like A&M and they'd had our number for a long time," said Thomas, remembering his senior season in 1995.

The Red Raiders hadn't beaten Texas A&M in six years, but the two rivals were tied 7-7 as the 1995 game entered the final minute of play at Jones Stadium in Lubbock.

"I faked like a blitz, and they kept Leeland McElroy (Aggies' running back) in to block," Thomas recalled. "So, on the next play, I faked blitz again."

McElroy stayed in to block, and Thomas stepped back into pass coverage, intercepting Cory Pullig's pass and returning it for a touchdown with just over thirty seconds remaining. The interception and subsequent score gave Texas Tech a 14-7 victory, certainly one of the great wins in Texas Tech football history.

"I've had other interceptions," Thomas said. "But the timing in that game in that rivalry was exciting. That was definitely one of my top plays in college. I appreciate Tech giving me the opportunity to live out my dream."

How could the Red Raiders top that 1995 finish? Well, a year later, they did—this time at Kyle Field in College Station. The Aggies were clinging to a 10-7 lead with just over six minutes remaining when Texas Tech took possession at its own nineteen-yard line.

Morris, a redshirt freshman running back in 1996, said he lined up as a slotback on the decisive play.

"I ran a wheel route, cut to the outside (behind two wide receivers who were running deep post routes) and then ran up the sideline," he remembered.

Morris said the pass from Zebbie Lethridge traveled about forty yards in the air. Morris hauled in the pass and raced down the sideline in front of the stunned Aggie Corps for an eighty-one-yard touchdown play.

"It's up there," responded Morris, when asked where his touchdown against A&M in 1996 ranks in his football career.

Six years later, history repeated itself as the Red Raiders and Aggies hooked up in a classic in front of 86,478 fans at Kyle Field, a thriller that Texas Tech won 48-47 in overtime. Tech fans, however, probably remember the game more for Welker's punt return late in the fourth quarter than what happened in overtime.

The Aggies were leading 34-31 when Welker gathered in a punt at Tech's twelve-yard line and raced eighty-eight yards for a touchdown to put the Raiders on top 38-34. Although the Aggies came back to score, Tech tied the game 41-41 with a last-second field goal and then won it in overtime.

"There was that famous picture of me running toward the end zone," Welker said. "You could see the Corps behind me and all the facial expressions."

Welker, who joined the New England Patriots in 2007, set an NCAA record with eight punt returns for touchdowns during his career at Texas Tech, but the eighty-eight-yarder against A&M in 2002 was his longest—and most memorable.

"That got my name out there," he said.

The three former Red Raiders teamed up for their first time full season together with the Dolphins in 2005, Miami's first year under new head coach Nick Saban, now at Alabama.

Welker said all three players still follow the Red Raiders closely. He said the three liked to harass the other Dolphin players from Big 12 schools during the week the Red Raiders play those teams. An obvious target is Miami's center, former Aggie Seth McKinney.

"We give 'em a little 'Guns Up' whenever we can," Morris said.

Texas' Top High School Football Coach

The greatest high school football coach in Texas history never played high school football himself.

Well, that is only partly true. Gordon Wood, a member of the graduating Class of 1934 at Abilene Wylie High School, actually played part of one season on the Abilene High B-team as a sophomore.

Wood who died at age eighty-nine in 2003 in Abilene just a few miles from where he was born, coached high school football for forty-three years. By the time he retired as the head football coach at Brownwood High School in 1985, Wood had won more games and more state championships than any coach in Texas high school football history. He has been honored by presidents and governors, been featured on national television and in *Sports Illustrated,* and has been selected to six different Halls of Fame. The *Dallas Morning News* named Wood the Texas High School "Coach of the Century" in 1999.

Although Celina High School coach G.A. Moore eventually passed Wood on the all-time wins list, Wood's nine state championships remain the standard for high school football coaches. Wood won two state titles at Stamford in the 1950s and captured seven more during an incredible twenty-six-year stint at Brownwood.

But back to the story of Wood's high school football "playing" career.

Wood said his family moved around from rented farm to rented farm around Abilene when he was growing up. He started school at Pleasant Hill, a one-room school located on property that is now part of Dyess Air Force Base, just west of Abilene.

When he was a seventh grader, Wood attended Central Elementary School in Abilene while his mother took a job working in town. There he received his first taste for football. The next year, he came back to Wylie, which was a country school about eight miles south of Abilene at the time and didn't field a football team. When he reached the tenth grade, Wood wanted to play football again.

"My love for football caused hard feelings between my father and me the year I entered the tenth grade," Wood wrote in his autobiography *Coach of the Century*. "I had decided I wanted to play football, but Dad was against it. He thought football was a waste of time. Wylie didn't have a football team, so I went behind Dad's back and talked my mother into transferring me to Abilene High School.

"That was the beginning of a confrontation—a confrontation I was bound to lose. Don't get me wrong. My father was a great guy—a hard worker, a good provider, an honest man. His word was as good as money in the bank, but Dad had strong convictions. Since I wouldn't be home to help with the other chores, Dad insisted I handle all the milking, every morning and every evening."

Wood said he caught a ride with Pug Cox, who lived at Buffalo Gap but was an all-state guard for Abilene High.

"Each morning after I milked the cows, I'd walk the mile and a half to Wylie and catch a ride with Pug," Wood said.

Wood played for Coach Dewey Mahew at Abilene High. He said Mahew was partial to long practices, and it was often 8 P.M. by the time Cox dropped him off at Wylie.

"I'd walk home and there would be all those cows to milk," Wood said. "I lasted eight weeks before I quit the Abilene football squad and transferred back to Wylie High. My father made his point. I never played another down of football all through high school.

Obviously, not having the opportunity to play high school football didn't prove to be a detriment to Wood's remarkable coaching career. His career record as a head football coach was 396-91-15.

From that humble beginning in which milking cows was far more important than playing football, came the man considered the greatest high school football coach in Texas history.

Parcells and Wood

Another Gordon Wood story.

Wood stayed active after his retirement at age seventy-one in 1985. One never went to a football game at the stadium that bears his name in Brownwood without seeing Wood sitting in the pressbox. It was not uncommon, either, to see Wood in a pressbox at Texas Stadium in Irving, Shotwell Stadium in Abilene or many other stadiums around the state during the high school playoffs.

Gordon Wood won nine State championships during his coaching career. Courtesy of Big Country Hall of Fame, Texas State Technical College, West Texas.

In 1999, the *Dallas Morning News* named him the "Coach of the Century." Wood co-wrote his autobiography *Coach of the Century* with Dallas author John Carver in 2001. In 2003, shortly before his death at age 89, Wood and Carver teamed up again to write a manual to help young coaches.

Wood was surprised in 1997, at age eighty-three, when he received unexpected praise from Bill Parcells, who was then the coach of the New York Jets. Parcells, later the head coach of the Dallas Cowboys, developed the reputation of being one of the great coaches in the National Football League during stops with the New York Giants, New England Patriots, Jets, and Cowboys.

Parcells, however, gives credit for his success to Wood, the legendary former Texas high school football coach.

"The story is not completely accurate," Wood said at the time. "But when you're eighty-three years old, you're happy when anybody is saying anything nice about you."

Wood learned of his influence on Parcells more than twenty years after their chance meeting. In fact, it was in the August 2, 1997, issue of the *New York Times* that columnist William C. Rhoden told the story of the first meeting between Parcells, then the coach of the Jets, and Wood.

"Parcells was the defensive coordinator at Texas Tech twenty years ago when he met Wood during spring practice," Rhoden wrote. "He noticed a 'rough-looking leathery kind of looking guy' wearing a maroon jacket with a 'B' on his cap. He came back, and came back, and came back."

"We had twenty spring practices," Parcells said. "I know he was there at least fifteen times, always down by the linebackers."

Parcells finally introduced himself to Wood, who said he coached in "a little town down the road here."

"Outside of Lubbock?" Parcells asked.

"No, a little further," Wood replied.

"I said, 'how far is it?'" Parcells recalled.

"Well, it's two-and-half hours (actually it is more like three-and-half hours from Brownwood to Lubbock) one way," Wood replied.

Parcells asked Wood if he stayed in a hotel, and Wood said no, he would drive up in the morning, watch practice, and then drive back home. Five hours or more each day on the road.

"And I knew he did it at least fifteen times, and at the time he had to be sixty years old," Parcells said.

Wood was actually sixty-three at the time. At the end of spring practice, Wood told Parcells he'd been watching him and thought he was a pretty good coach. Then he peppered Parcells with questions.

"He asked why are you teaching this, show me how you do that," Parcells said. "Here is a guy who never lost, he never ever lost. I think of him every season when we start. I think about this guy.

"He doesn't even know me. I don't know him. I only crossed paths with him one year, but he was very influential on me. The guy's fifty-eight, sixty years old, won 300-something games, and is driving five hours a day to find out something."

Wood admitted he and Parcells never again talked after their initial meeting at spring practice in Lubbock in 1977.

Someone in Manchester, New Hampshire, called Wood the day after the story ran in the *New York Times* to tell him about it and then sent him the article. Rhoden's telling of the story is not original, however. It also appears in Parcells' book *Finding A Way to Win*, published in 1995. Wood said he found out about the book by accident a year later.

"Katharine (Wood's wife) didn't go to church one Sunday and she was listening to a preacher out of Dallas," Wood said. "He used that story in his sermon. I wondered where in the world he got that story."

Wood called the church and found out that the story was in Parcells' book, which Wood then purchased.

Since their meeting in 1977, both certainly had success. Wood won two more state titles at Brownwood and reached the championship game one other time, giving him a record nine state championships before retiring in 1985.

Parcells, meanwhile, won two Super Bowl titles with the Giants and took the Patriots to another Super Bowl.

Wood, who received numerous awards and accolades during his unparalleled career as a Texas high school football coach, was thrilled at age eighty-three to learn his influence extended beyond the thousands of players who had played for him.

Parcells, one of the great coaches in NFL history, claimed Wood had as great an influence on him as "Halas, Lombardi, Noll and Landry."

He Did It His Way

I will never forget the first time I interviewed Bob Knight. It was long before "The General" came to Texas Tech and became the winningest college men's basketball coach in history.

It was in the fall of 1992, and Knight, then coaching at Indiana University, came to Abilene to recruit Andrae Patterson, a talented 6'9" forward from Abilene Cooper, who became Mr. Basketball in Texas as a senior in 1994, a *Parade* All-American that year, and eventually played four seasons for Knight with the Hoosiers.

A one-on-one interview with Knight can be intimidating. One, he doesn't grant many and turned down all three television sta-

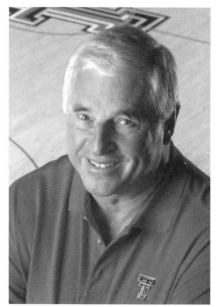

Texas Tech Coach Bob Knight.
Courtesy of Texas Tech sports information department.

tions in Abilene that same day that I talked to him for the first time. A friendship with Dan Dakich, an assistant at IU who later became the head coach at Bowling Green, had paved the way for my "exclusive" interview. And two, Knight is the closest thing to a "larger-than-life" presence of anyone I have met. He can be an intimidating figure.

Knowing Knight couldn't talk about Patterson (NCAA rules forbid a coach to discuss a potential recruit with the media), I steered our conversation to the 1984 Olympics. Knight had coached a U.S. team that included North Carolina's Michael Jordan to a gold medal in Los Angeles that summer. Jordan and the Chicago Bulls had just won another NBA title several months prior to our 1992 interview.

"Did you realize that Jordan was going to become the greatest player in the game?" I asked Knight. "Coming out of that team concept at North Carolina, I don't think most of us realized just how good he was going to be."

"Most of you don't realize a whole hell of a lot," replied Knight, who then went on to politely answer my question.

It was classic Knight, who used the opportunity to make sure he put me in my place before we got too far into the interview. After that, he was very cordial. In fact, when our interview finished, he asked me lots of questions about Abilene, the high schools in town, the economy of the town, etc. I even discovered his father was born in Arkansas near where I once lived.

All in all, it was one of the most fascinating interviews I have ever conducted. I have interviewed him at least a half dozen other times in the years that followed. But little did I dream that more than fourteen years later, Knight would capture career victory No. 880, surpassing North Carolina's Dean Smith as the coach with the most wins in NCAA Division I men's college basketball.

And, to think, Knight did it in Texas—a state better known for its football—on New Year's Day, a date normally reserved for college football bowl games. Knight achieved victory No. 880 on January 1, 2007, in front of a packed house at the United Spirit Arena in Lubbock as Texas Tech edged New Mexico 70-68.

As the on-court postgame ceremony, including tributes from other coaches and ex-players, concluded, Frank Sinatra's "I Did It My Way" blared over the loudspeakers in the United Spirit Arena. Even Knight, in his postgame press conference, admitted that was a good choice for a song depicting his career.

His volatile personality has often gotten him into trouble. From throwing a chair to being accused of choking a player,

Knight's temper cost him his job at Indiana. Yet, for all the criticism he seems to bring on himself, there is that other side of Knight. Not only he is now the college basketball's winningest coach but he has never been accused of any recruiting scandals.

His track record with the NCAA is squeaky clean. He has won over a forty-one-year career that spans parts of five decades at three different schools with entirely different recruiting challenges—West Point, Indiana, and Texas Tech. The graduation rate of the players he has coached is among the best in the nation, and he has raised thousands of dollars—much out of his own pocket—for the libraries at both Indiana and Texas Tech.

Bob Knight at Texas Tech's United Spirit Arena. Courtesy of Texas Tech sports information department.

"I don't expect you people to have agreed with what I've done—and if I did (care), I would have asked your opinion," Knight said in the postgame press conference after his record-breaking victory. "And I have never asked the opinions of very many. I've simply tried to do what I think is best in the way that I think you have to do it. I think I've put myself out on a limb at times, knowingly, simply because I thought what I was going to do or say was the best way to get this kid to be the best player or the best student."

For all his dichotomy of personal attributes, there is much to admire. Even from a coach whose first response to my initial interview with him was "Most of you don't realize a whole hell of a lot."

He may have been right, but most people wouldn't have said it. Bob Knight is not most people.

The Winningest Girls Basketball Coach

ob Knight is not the only record-setting basketball coach in Texas. Leta Andrews of Granbury holds the distinction of being the winningest girls' basketball coach in the nation. Sometime during the 2007-2008 season, she will pass former Fort Worth Dunbar coach Robert Hughes and become the all-time leader in wins for a high school basketball coach in Texas—male or female.

Andrews, who turned seventy in July 2007, shows no signs of slowing down.

"I'm taking it one year at time," she said. "I'm a 5K runner, and I still do that. My family is very supportive, and I'm still in good health."

And she is still winning basketball games. Andrews, who started her coaching career in 1962, has won 1,256 games and lost just 236 in forty-five seasons on the bench. Consider this: she has 1,020 more victories than losses, and she has averaged 27.9 wins per season. Not bad for someone who originally didn't plan to coach.

Andrews, who played on a state finalist basketball team at Granbury, received her degree in elementary education from Texas Wesleyan.

"I did my practice teaching, and that's when I decided that was not what I wanted to do," she said. "We were starving to death as a family (she and her husband had two small daughters at the time), but I went back to school to get my teaching certificate so I could coach."

Andrews landed her first job in tiny Tolar. Coaching stints followed at Gustine, Comanche and Calallen before returning to her hometown in 1992.

"Every stop holds loads of good memories," she said.

And lots of wins.

"One of my greatest thrills is my love for my young ladies and the game of basketball," she added. "I have sat at the feet of some of the greatest basketball minds ever."

Girls basketball was just in its infancy when Andrews started coaching, so she attended clinics conducted by the top men's coaches such as Adolph Rupp, John Wooden and Dean Smith to try to learn more about the game. She still visits with Wooden on the telephone.

"When women's basketball developed, I studied under coaches like Jody Conradt and Pat Summitt," she continued.

Andrews also made the transition from the girls' half-court six-on-six game the first sixteen years of her coaching career to the five-on-five full-court game the girls play today.

"I fought to keep the six-on-six game because I thought everyone couldn't shoot the basketball," she said. "The baseline-to-baseline game is a tough game. But it is better now."

Andrews' only state championship came in 1990 when she was coaching at Calallen.

"Any highlight is a state championship," she said. "But every day I work with my young ladies is highlight. I don't want to miss a thing. I have been blessed with so many awards. It makes me think how I want to live my life. I want to be a strong leader in my school and my community."

She admitted it is difficult to motivate today's players in comparison to the earlier days of coaching career.

"It is difficult to get them to have the same work ethic," Andrews said. "It very much is a different way of life today. The young ladies have so many distractions, and so many other things to do."

Granbury's Jia Perkins, who went on to star at Texas Tech, is one of the top players Andrews coached.

"Jia would be right at the top," she said, "but Linda (Andrews' daughter) was a good player, too. She played for Coach Conradt at Texas and is in their Hall of Fame. She scored forty-two points one night for me (at Comanche) and missed only one shot."

In March 2007 at the McDonald's High School All-America Game in Louisville, Kentucky, Andrews was recognized for her remarkable career. The Naismith Memorial Basketball Hall of Fame named Jack Curran of Archbishop Molloy High School in Briarwood, New York, and Andrews as the inaugural recipients of the Morgan Wootten Award for lifetime achievement in coaching high school basketball.

Wootten, the first and only coach to be elected to the Naismith Memorial Basketball Hall of Fame as a result of his high school coaching achievements, won 1,274 games in forty-six seasons at DeMatha High School in Maryland.

His record for career wins may soon be passed by the girls basketball coach from Granbury, Texas.

"I'm a very blessed individual," Andrews noted.

Miller:
A Division III Success Story

They toil in relative obscurity compared to their Division I counterparts like Mack Brown, Bob Knight, Billy Gillispie, Rick Barnes, Augie Garrido and Larry Hays at schools such as Texas, Texas A&M and Texas Tech.

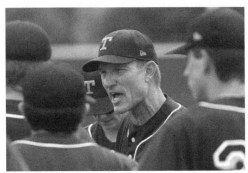

Former Texas Lutheran baseball Coach Bill Miller. Courtesy of Drew Engelke.

But Texas has numerous Division III coaches who have amassed remarkable records. For those unfamiliar with NCAA Division III, it is a division made up of primarily small private schools that don't offer athletic scholarships. Instead, athletes come to school, paying their own high tuition just for the chance to continue to compete at the collegiate level. The American Southwest Conference is a fifteen-member Division III league that encompasses four states, including twelve schools in Texas.

The standard-bearer for the state's Division III coaches was Texas Lutheran University baseball coach Bill Miller, who announced his retirement from coaching following the 2007 season to become the school's full-time athletic director. Miller reached career victory No. 500 in the spring of 2007 with a 9-3 win over Southwestern University.

Five days later, Miller's Bulldogs swept a doubleheader from the University of Ozarks, giving him career wins No. 502 and 503. That eclipsed the school record of 502 wins by Miller's mentor and former coach, Ray Katt, who retired in 1992 after 22 seasons as the head baseball coach at TLU with 502 wins, 362 losses and two ties.

Miller, who succeeded Katt at Texas Lutheran in Seguin, downplays his accomplishment, however.

"The bottom line in baseball, you've got to have good players to have a chance to win," he said. "Coaching in baseball is important, but kids come in here with a good baseball background. Kids made good decisions, and I've been fortunate to have good players."

When asked to name several highlights of his career, Miller remembered his last two teams that won back-to-back ASC titles and advanced to the NCAA Division III West Regional finals both years.

"For me, it was games that allowed us to win championships," he said. "The last two years we won the conference tournament and played well in the regional. I also remember the battles we used to have with St. Mary's (when Texas Lutheran was Division II in the Heart of Texas Conference). In 1999 we had a good team and won the conference title on the last weekend against St. Edward's. Of course, the two years we beat the University of Texas back-to-back was exciting for our university."

Miller's Bulldogs shocked the Longhorns, winning back-to-back games over Texas in 1996 and 1997.

He began his coaching career at Spring Woods, where he was an assistant coach for a high school team that included future Hall of Fame pitcher Roger Clemens and Rayner Noble, now the head baseball coach at the University of Houston. Miller was then the head coach at Converse Judson before returning to Texas Lutheran to replace Katt.

Miller retired with a combined high school and college coaching record of 655-241-3 (530-191-3 in fifteen seasons at Texas

Lutheran and 125-50 in seven years at Converse Judson High School). That is an overall winning percentage of .730. His first season at Converse Judson was his only losing season in twenty-two years. His teams won at least thirty games in fourteen of his fifteen seasons at Texas Lutheran and won three consecutive conference championships to close out his career.

Coach Bill Miller tries to make his point with an umpire. Courtesy of Drew Engelke.

"At schools like Texas Lutheran and the other Division III team in our league, academics are really important," he added. "To do this and graduate players, the university has been supportive of me and our program. You have to have that. Give credit to the administration. But it comes down to players. I really believe that."

Miller, and many other outstanding coaches on the college level in Texas, have found not only good players but also success both on the field or court and in molding young people's lives in the relative obscurity of small private universities playing on the NCAA Division III level.

Teammates in the
"Game of the Century"

Collegefootball seemingly has a "Game of the Century" every few years now, but one contest that has stood the test of time and is still considered one of the greatest games played in the last century was the 1971 Thanksgiving Day game between Oklahoma and Nebraska at Owen Field in Norman, Oklahoma.

Books have been written and television documentaries produced about that game. Maybe best remembered for Johnny Rodgers' spectacular punt return for the Cornhuskers, the match up featured the Oklahoma wishbone, an unstoppable offensive attack that allowed the Sooners to become the most prolific rushing team in college football history, setting a NCAA rushing record of 472 yards per game that season, a mark that still stands today. OU quarterback Jack Mildren ran for 1,140 yards himself that season, a record for quarterbacks.

Nebraska was the defending national champion in 1971, and the Cornhuskers had been ranked No. 1 and Oklahoma No. 2 for seven weeks. Both teams were undefeated going into the Thanksgiving Day showdown. Prior to the kickoff, the Huskers had been invited to the Orange Bowl in Miami and a shot at the national championship against Alabama. The Sooners were invited to the Sugar Bowl.

It was billed as the "Game of the Century," and it turned out to be one of the rare instances—much like the University of Texas' win over Southern California in the 2006 Rose Bowl—where the game proved to be even better than the enormous pre-game hype.

The largest viewing audience in the history of college football at the time tuned in on Thanksgiving afternoon as ABC sent a live telecast via satellite around the world. Fans saw the lead change hands four times before Nebraska won a 35-31 thriller.

What may have been forgotten about that game is that former high school teammates from Texas nearly pulled out the victory for Oklahoma.

Jack Mildren, who went on to a NFL career and later became lieutenant governor of Oklahoma, and wide receiver Jon Harrison had been teammates on an Abilene Cooper team that lost a last-second heartbreaker to Austin Reagan in the Class 4A state championship game in 1967. Mildren went directly to Oklahoma as a highly touted quarterback, but Harrison played football for two years at Northeastern Oklahoma A&M in Miami, Oklahoma, where he was the most valuable player in the national championship game as NEO captured a national junior college championship. But here they were together again in OU uniforms on an even bigger stage in 1971.

"I caught 78 passes (for 1,280 yards and fifteen touchdowns) my senior year in high school (still a Cooper school record)," Harrison said. "But I was on Jack's coattails. I never even knew I was good enough to play at that level until my senior year in high school. Oklahoma saw me when they were recruiting Jack."

Harrison, normally relegated to a blocker for Oklahoma's wishbone running game, had his greatest game as a receiver against the Cornhuskers, hauling in four passes for 115 yards and two touchdowns. His thirty-two-yard catch set up OU's first field goal. He also completed a fifty-one-yard pass off an end-around reverse.

"I had probably only thrown that two times in practice," Harrison recalled. "We had Willie Franklin, who was a champion javelin thrower, and he usually threw it when we ran the reverse. But I completed it to Albert Chandler down to the twelve- or fifteen-yard line to set up a score."

Nebraska did a pretty good job of shutting down halfback Greg Pruitt in Oklahoma's wishbone running game that day, but Mildren surprised the No. 1-ranked Cornhuskers by running for 130 yards and passing for 137 more, including the two touchdowns to his former high school teammate.

Thanks to Rodgers' spectacular seventy-two-yard punt return, Nebraska jumped out to a 14-3 lead. But Oklahoma scored to cut it to 14-10, and Mildren then drove the Sooners seventy-eight yards in forty-six seconds, hitting Harrison on a twenty-four-yard TD pass with five seconds remaining before halftime to give OU a 17-14 lead.

"Our coaches were coming out of the press box, and they told Jack to just run out the clock," Harrison said.

Instead, Mildren found Harrison open for a forty-three-yard completion and then hooked up with Harrison again for the go-ahead scoring strike.

The two teams then traded touchdowns in the second half as the lead see-sawed back-and-forth. The Huskers went up 21-17 on Jeff Kinney's three-yard run, but Oklahoma answered with a score to regain the lead 24-17.

Another short plunge by Kinney with twenty-eight seconds left in the third quarter put Nebraska back in front 28-24. But Oklahoma responded with a seventeen-yard touchdown pass from Mildren to Harrison to take a 31-28 advantage with 7:10 showing on the clock.

Nebraska came right back with a perfectly executed time-consuming march, climaxed by Kinney's fourth touchdown of the day, a two-yard dive with 1:38 remaining that gave the Cornhuskers the dramatic 35-31 victory.

The script for one of the greatest games in college football history would have had a much different ending, however, if Mildren's final pass to Harrison in the closing seconds would have been three or four inches shorter.

"I was running a post route, and I was wide open," Harrison said. "They were playing man-to-man coverage, and I probably made too good of a move. I got too far outside, and I hit the cornerback when I jumped back inside. That bump slowed me down just enough that the pass went off my fingertips."

Despite being a wide receiver on a team that seldom threw the football, Harrison certainly made his mark at Oklahoma. *Sooner Spectator* magazine recently ranked him as the number three receiver in OU football history. In his two seasons in Norman, Harrison had thirty catches for 811 yards and six touchdowns. That is an average of 27 yards per reception, which is still the school record today. Harrison also averaged 29.7 yards on 17 catches in 1971, which also remains the Sooners' single-season record.

Harrison, who has spent seventeen years as an assistant football and baseball coach at his alma mater, Abilene Cooper, before retiring following the 2006-2007 school year, said he is still asked about the game by fans.

"There is no telling how many people watched that game on TV," he added.

The "Game of the Century," remembered by football fans everywhere, has folklore status in Nebraska. But think how differently it would be remembered today if two Texas high school teammates, who enjoyed one of their finest games on college football's biggest stage, would have connected on that final pass on Thanksgiving Day 1971.

If he would have caught that final pass, *Sooner Spectator* magazine might have had Jon Harrison ranked number one on its all-time list.

Harrison: A Man of Firsts

When Chuck Harrison was inducted into the Big Country Athletic Hall of Fame in 2006 in his hometown of Abilene, he told the audience that a play in which he was involved during his professional baseball career had been written up in *The Sporting News*, known then as the "Bible of Baseball."

Playing for Richmond in an International League game at Buffalo in 1968, Harrison said he recorded two assists and a putout on the same play. Could anyone describe what happened? No, it didn't involve a rundown. Give up? Well, he stumped the audience that night, too.

Harrison was playing first base for the Atlanta Braves' Triple-A team in Richmond. Buffalo had the bases loaded when the Bisons' batter hit a grounder to Harrison.

He tossed the ball to the pitcher covering first base. The pitcher dropped the ball, however, allowing the runner to score from third. By the time Harrison recovered the ball that had bounced away from the pitcher, the runner on second was trying to score. Harrison threw home, but the runner slid into the catcher and knocked the ball loose. It caromed back toward first base, and Harrison retrieved it again. By now, the runner who had begun the play on first base was trying to score, too. Harrison outran the base runner to home plate and tagged him out to end the bizarre play.

For those of you scoring at home, that was 3-to-1-to-3-to-2-to-3.

You don't see that very often.

Chuck Harrison's 1967 Houston Astros baseball card.

But Harrison's career was full of "firsts." He was the first Texas Tech player to make the major leagues. He played for the Houston Astros in the first season in the Astrodome, and he was the starting first baseman in the first game ever played by the expansion Kansas City Royals. But that wasn't all.

Harrison, who was a member of state championship teams in both football and baseball at Abilene High, went to Texas Tech to play both sports. He said playing in the Red Raiders' first football game in the Southwest Conference was one of the highlights of his career in Lubbock.

"That was a huge deal then," he said. "It was a big thing playing in that first game."

Harrison started at defensive end as a sophomore, playing in front of all-American linebacker E.J. Holub.

"My job was to stop the reverse and hold up the end so E.J. could make the tackle," he quipped. "Nobody ever ran at E.J. The next year they moved me to center to replace E.J."

Harrison suffered a neck injury as a junior, which helped him decide to give up his football career and concentrate on baseball. He left college after his junior year to sign with the Astros.

During his junior baseball season at Tech, however, Harrison sported a 1.020 slugging percentage—meaning he hit for more bases than at-bats. That mark stood as an NCAA record for twenty years.

Harrison led the Texas League with forty home runs in 1964 while playing for the San Antonio Bullets. Playing on a Texas League championship team that included Joe Morgan, Sonny Jackson, and Chris Zachary, Harrison also led the league in total bases with 297 and was second in the league with 119 runs batted-in.

It wasn't until September of the following season in 1965 that he finally received a call-up to the Astros, however, allowing him to play in that inaugural season in the Astrodome, then known as the "Eighth Wonder of the World" as the first home to indoor baseball. Although he hit twenty-three doubles and nine home runs in his first full rookie season the following year with Houston in 1966, Harrison was not a fan of the Astrodome, where the real grass turned brown without sunlight and fly balls were lost looking up toward the roof.

"That was the worst place in the world," he said. "Half of those doubles would have been home runs in any other park."

The Astrodome was cavernous. When the Dome first opened, it was 340 feet down each line, 375 to the power alleys and 406 feet to straightaway center field. And the ball didn't carry well with the air conditioning blowing in from the outfield.

Harrison said he expected to be the Astros' every-day first baseman in 1967. Houston general manager Paul Richards, however, traded for veteran Hall-of-Famer and Texarkana native Eddie Matthews. Harrison and Matthews platooned at first base that year, with the left-handed-swinging Matthews batting against right-handers and the right-handed-hitting Harrison facing southpaws.

"Except when we played the Cardinals," Harrison explained. "If we were facing Bob Gibson, I'd come into the locker room and Eddie would be up on the training table. He'd say, 'My back is hurting, rookie. You'll have to play today.'"

But Matthews received most of the playing time that season, appearing in 101 games through mid-August. Part of the reason the Astros acquired Matthews was for the publicity as he approached his 500th career home run.

"He started the year with 493," Harrison said. "But he couldn't hit one out of the Astrodome. He didn't get his 500th homer until August 15. Immediately after that, they traded him to Detroit. He hit nine more homers in the last month-and-half of the season with the Tigers."

Matthews belted only three more long balls in thirty-one games with Detroit the next season in 1968 before officially retiring with 512 career home runs.

Harrison was traded to Atlanta and spent the 1968 season playing at Richmond. The expansion Kansas City Royals acquired him during the off-season, and he was the Royals' starting first baseman in the franchise's first game in 1969.

He played just parts of the 1969 and 1971 seasons with the Royals, alternating between Kansas City and their Triple-A affiliate in Omaha. Despite his impressive home run numbers in the minor leagues, Harrison finished his five-year major league career with just seventeen home runs, a victim of having to platoon and playing in the Astrodome and Kansas City's old Municipal Stadium, both tough home-run parks for right-handed hitters.

Few athletes, however, can match all the "firsts" that Harrison accumulated in his career.

Almost Perfect

A perfect game—retiring all twenty-seven batters in nine innings without allowing a base runner—is considered the rarest feat in baseball. It has happened only fifteen times since 1900 in major league baseball.

Abilene native John Lackey narrowly missed perfection in the 2006 season, instead accomplishing a baseball oddity even more unusual than a perfect game. The tall Los Angeles Angels right-hander gave up a leadoff double in the bottom of the first inning to Oakland A's centerfielder Mark Kotsay on July 7, 2006, and then retired the next twenty-seven batters in a row to record a shutout in the Angels' 3-0 victory.

"It just turned out to be a shutout," the 6'6", 235-pound Lackey told MLB.com after the game in downplaying his performance. "I didn't get it done."

Actually, it was much more than just a shutout. Lackey's effort was the eleventh one-hitter of the 2006 baseball season. It was also only the fourth time since 1950 that a pitcher has spun such an oddity, giving up a leadoff hit and then retiring twenty-seven in a row. It was the first such "unusual" one-hitter since Jerry Reuss did it for the Dodgers in an 11-1 win over the Cincinnati Reds on June 11, 1982.

"I think Lackey is throwing the ball as well as anyone in the game today," Angels manager Mike Scioscia said. "There have been a lot of games when a guy has great stuff but he gives up eight hits. Twenty-seven outs in a row is special, there is no doubt about it."

Lackey's gem came in the middle of a remarkable stretch in July in which he hurled 31 consecutive scoreless innings. His effort earned Lackey the American League pitcher of the month award.

Achieving the unusual is nothing new for Lackey, a three-sport standout at Abilene High School who oddly enough didn't become a pitcher until he attended Grayson County College. In 2002, he became the first rookie pitcher to win a Game Seven of the World Series since Babe Adams for the 1909 Pittsburgh Pirates.

"No, man, that was for a ring," Lackey responded when asked to compare his near-perfect game with his Game Seven win in the 2002 World Series. "But I do feel I pitched well."

Brotherhood of Indian Belly-Landing Experts

What would have happened to Baylor football if Grant Teaff had never coached the Bears? Teaff won 128 games in twenty-one seasons as the most successful coach in school history, guiding the Bears to a pair of Southwest Conference championships. He was a six-time SWC Coach of the Year and once won the national coach of the year award.

How would the college football coaching profession be different if Teaff, now the executive director of the American Football Coaches Association, hadn't come along?

How different would McMurry University basketball have been if Hershel Kimbrell hadn't coached the Indians? He won 448 games in thirty-one seasons as McMurry's men's basketball coach, earning selection to the NAIA Hall of Fame and Big Country Athletic Hall of Fame.

Tampa Bay Storm coach Tim Marcum has more career victories than any other coach in Arena Football League history,

1963 McMurry Indians Football Team. Courtesy of McMurry University.

including a record seven ArenaBowl titles. How different would that league have been if Marcum had never coached?

Clovis Hale was a long-time assistant coach at Texas Tech. Bill Grissom, Ken Bode, James Christopher, Waco Reynolds, Winford Shipp, Doyle Slaton, and Dick Spier all became successful high school football coaches in Texas. How many young people's lives did they help mold during their coaching careers?

Coach Hershel Kimbrell talks to McMurry faculty after safely landing in Abilene. Courtesy of McMurry University.

Had it not been for a twist of fate more than forty years ago, however, none of those coaches would have had the careers they enjoyed or influenced the lives they did.

It was September 28, 1963, and Teaff, a young coach in his first college head coaching position at McMurry, was anxious to get home after his Indians had suffered a tough 8-7 loss to Northeast Louisiana State on a controversial call late in the game.

Twenty-eight players, three coaches, two pilots, and a stewardess boarded a DC-3 in Monroe, Louisiana, for the return trip to Abilene. The plane had a difficult time taking off, however, barely making it off the runway and just clipping the top of several trees at the end of the runway.

"We were told later that they lock the elevators (that give the plane lift, enabling it to get off the ground) down when a plane is parked on the runway," said Grissom, who was a senior on the Indians' team that fall. "They forgot to unlock the elevators."

Realizing the problem, the pilot tried to land the plane twice at the Monroe airport. The first time the plane hit hard and blew out a tire, bending the landing gear. The second time, without a left landing gear, the plane's left wing touched the runway. But the pilot was able to get the DC-3 airborne again.

With a damaged landing gear, electrical system damage, and the plane full of fuel, the crew decided to try a belly-landing at Barksdale Air Force Base near Shreveport.

After a forty-minute, low-level flight in darkness to the Air Force base, the team had plenty of time to wonder about their lives and what might happen next.

"Going over there was a unique time," said Teaff, who wrote about the incident in his book *I Believe*, published in 1975. "First of all, we all face death every day, but you don't put it into a compact package where you've just gone through three opportunities—a takeoff and two landings—to die, and now you're going in for another."

Kimbrell later said their flight was so low over the small towns between Monroe and Shreveport in northern Louisiana that he was able to watch "Gunsmoke" on television through the windows of the houses they passed over.

Coach Grant Teaff with his family after landing safely in Abilene. Courtesy of McMurry University.

The pilots had radioed Barksdale AFB to ask that the runway be foamed down to aid a crash landing. But, for whatever reason, when the plane touched down there was no foam. The right prop dug into the concrete, tore away from the plane and sailed off. The right engine burst into flames, and the right wing started to burn.

"I can still see it like it happened yesterday," Grissom said. "They told us to keep our head between our legs. But it was such a shock the first time we hit that you couldn't help but look up. I looked out the window, and there was a big ol' ball of fire coming off the runway. We would hit and bounce like a skipping rock across a tank until we finally came to stop. I can still see it in my mind. I don't know why the fuel tanks didn't explode."

When the plane finally came to a stop, assistant coach Buddy Fornes kicked open a door and everyone on board got off the plane safely in less than thirty seconds.

"The plane was a wreck, a terrible mess," Teaff wrote in his book. "The fire chief said he's never seen a plane so hot fail to explode."

After returning to Abilene, the team held a meeting and decided to form a club, the Brotherhood of Indian Belly-Landing Experts (B.I.B.L.E.). The group has held reunions every five or ten years. Grissom still carries a well-worn B.I.B.L.E. card in his billfold with a list of everyone who was on the plane that night.

The aircraft with a wrecked propeller. Courtesy of McMurry University.

The card also lists a scripture, Romans 8:31: "What shall we then say to these things? If God be for us, who can be against us?"

"It could have taken most of the lives on board," said Grissom, who is now retired after spending thirty-five years as a successful high school head football coach in West Texas at Hamlin, Breckenridge, Stanton, Colorado City and Coleman. "But God had something else planned for those guys. A lot of guys turned out to be coaches and successful businessmen."

It was a fateful night when the members of the Brotherhood of Indian Belly-Landing Experts faced death together.

"I was convinced we had been spared by God for a reason," Teaff said at the twenty-fifth reunion of the group. "There was a reason why we were able to walk away from that. And that's what I tried to tell them then—what were they going to do with it? It heightened my faith and Christian beliefs. Those beliefs are so interspersed with who I am and what I am. Without a question, it made me better in every area. I'm a better father, better coach, better Christian. I don't think there is any question it had a profound effect on me."

Baseball's Best
Right-Handed Hitter

A most unusual reunion was held on April 20, 1996, at The Ballpark in Arlington.

A family reunion at a baseball game might not seem that out of the ordinary, but this event involved the four grandchildren of Rogers Hornsby, the native Texan who is generally regarded as the greatest right-handed hitter in baseball history. The four were recognized in pregame ceremonies to celebrate the 100th anniversary of Hornsby's birth.

But the unique feature of this reunion was that it marked the first time the four grandchildren had all met each other. One lived in Denison, two in Tennessee and one in Virginia.

So why had Hornsby's grandchildren never met?

Hornsby had two sons by two different wives. He became estranged from his sons, and the grandchildren had never met until that 1996 reunion in Arlington.

The nation's leading authority on Hornsby is Charles Alexander, who first became a fan of the baseball legend when, at age fourteen, he spent much of the summer of 1950 at the ballpark in Beaumont. The Beaumont team, a New York Yankees' minor league affiliate, and had hired Hornsby as team manager that summer. Fueled by an influx of young talent provided by the Yankees, including future star infielder Gil McDougald, Beaumont won its first Texas League championship that year.

"It was one of the great summers of my life," Alexander said. "I have very vivid memories of that summer. It is stamped on my memory forever."

Alexander, a noted baseball biographer and a professor at Ohio University, in Athens, Ohio, where he teaches a class on the history of baseball, published a book *Rogers Hornsby: A Biography* in conjunction with the 100th anniversary of Hornsby's birth and presented a lecture on Hornsby's life at The Legends of the Game Baseball Museum that weekend at The Ballpark.

"This is the third biography I've written," Alexander noted that weekend. "I've written biographies on Ty Cobb and John McGraw, so I've been working in that vain of history. I'm interested in controversial and complex biographical subjects. It was fascinating and as much fun for me as McGraw and Cobb."

Alexander said he tracked Hornsby's life through public records, the *Sporting News*, and daily newspaper accounts.

"Hornsby was in baseball until his death in 1963," he said, "and he managed in the majors in 1952 and 1953, so there are a lot of players still alive who played for him. I interviewed many of them."

Alexander also made his first visit to West Texas to find Hornsby's birthplace in the small town of Winters.

"I went to the Runnels County courthouse in Ballinger," he said, "and went through the deeds. I was able to find the location where he was born."

Alexander said there is nothing there now but a pasture, just west of Winters, on the farm where Hornsby was born. Although there is no evidence that Hornsby ever returned to Winters after he left at age two or three, Winters does have a museum in honor of its most famous native son.

Hornsby's roots run about as deep in Texas as one can imagine. His great-great grandfather was among the first white settlers in Travis County, and Hornsby is buried in the family cemetery at Hornsby Bend on the Colorado River, just east of Austin.

With farm land becoming hard to find in Travis County, Hornsby's father and mother moved to Winters in 1895, looking for new opportunities. The next year, Rogers was born, the youngest of five Hornsby children. His father died when Rogers was only two or three, however, so his mother moved the family back to Travis County.

Several years later, when Swift and Armour opened its meat-packing plants in Fort Worth, the Hornsby family moved there to seek new job opportunities. Rogers grew up in Fort Worth. His older brothers worked in the packing plants, and Rogers played for the stockyards' baseball team. But Rogers was destined to become a baseball player, not a worker in a packing plant. He attended high school at Fort Worth Northside but dropped out after his sophomore year to pursue a career in baseball.

"He was a very difficult person," Alexander said. "He was a hard-nosed baseball man, and a hard-nosed person otherwise. He had no patience with the frivolous side of life. His range of interests was limited to baseball, gambling on horses, and women."

Alexander said Hornsby was married three times—and a "long-time companion" committed suicide by jumping out of a hotel room window in Chicago. Hornsby had two sons by different marriages.

Rogers Jr. became estranged from his father when his parents divorced in 1923. He was raised by his mother and stepfather in Denison, where Hornsby's professional baseball career first began.

"To my knowledge, Rogers Jr. never saw his father after he was three-and-a-half years old; he was killed in an Air Force bomber accident in 1949," Alexander explained.

Hornsby's other son, Billy, played minor league baseball briefly, but never made it to the big leagues. When his baseball career failed, Billy bought into a beer distributorship. Hornsby didn't drink and disapproved of his son's business, so they, too, became separated. Billy died in 1983.

So the four grandchildren had never all been together until that weekend in Arlington. Although they never knew their grandfather, they certainly learned what an amazing baseball player he was. Considered the greatest right-handed hitter of all-time, Hornsby batted .300 or better in fourteen of his twenty-three big-league seasons and won seven National League batting titles.

He approached his craft with the utmost intensity and many idiosyncrasies. He didn't drink or smoke. He never played golf, and he even refused to read books or see movies for fear of hurting his eyesight. It must have paid off because his .358 career batting average ranks second only to Ty Cobb's .366 career mark.

Hornsby, elected to the National Baseball Hall of Fame in Cooperstown, New York, in 1942, is the only right-hander to bat .400 or better in three different seasons. He holds the modern-day record for the highest single-season batting average of .424 in 1924.

He also won 1,530 games in fifteen seasons as a major league manager. He lived most of his life in St. Louis and Chicago, where he had played the majority of his twenty-three-year big league career for the Cardinals and Cubs.

"But he always maintained ties to Texas," Alexander said.

Hornsby managed in the minors twice in Texas—in Fort Worth in 1942 and Beaumont in 1950.

Catching the Oldest Rookie

Sports fans probably had never heard of Lance Hardin, but, thanks to a popular movie, they learned about the role he played in one of the most fascinating baseball stories to come along in many years.

Hardin had just graduated from De Leon High School, a small town about halfway between Fort Worth and Abilene, in 2001 when he decided to attend a Tampa Bay Devil Rays' tryout camp at Howard Payne University in Brownwood.

"I just wanted to see what a pro tryout was like," said Hardin, who was a second-team Class 2A all-state selection at catcher at De Leon and later spent a couple of seasons on the baseball team at Tarleton State.

The story of that tryout camp has been retold in the critically acclaimed book *The Oldest Rookie*. Disney then turned the book into the movie *The Rookie*, starring Dennis Quaid, which won an ESPY award as the top sports movie in 2002.

Jimmy Morris was coaching at Reagan County High School in Big Lake, west of San Angelo, in the spring of 1999. His team made him promise that if it won the first district baseball championship in school history that Coach Morris would go to a baseball tryout camp.

Morris had graduated from high school in Brownwood, where he played football for legendary coach Gordon Wood. But the Lions didn't have a high school baseball team in those days. Morris went to Ranger College to play baseball and was drafted by the Milwaukee Brewers in 1983.

He spent six years as a left-handed pitcher in the Brewers' minor league system, never reaching higher than the Class A level. Five surgeries on his elbow and shoulder later—including the "Tommy John surgery" in which a tendon from his ankle was transplanted into his elbow—Morris gave up his dream and quit baseball in 1989.

Morris went back to school, completing his degree at Angelo State. He then coached for one year at Haskell before taking a job as an assistant football coach and head baseball coach at Reagan County.

In his second year at Reagan County, the Owls won their first district baseball championship, and Morris had to honor his promise he had made to his team to make another try at a professional baseball career.

It had been ten years since he had retired from baseball, and he knew no baseball team would give a thirty-five-year-old a try-out. But Morris went to a Tampa Bay Devil Rays' tryout camp in Brownwood on that Saturday in early June anyway, just to keep his promise to his team.

If you've seen the movie, you'll remember the factual scene in which Morris takes his three small children (one in a stroller) with him to sign up for the tryout camp.

"Bringing your kids to try out?" Doug Gasaway, a Devil Rays' scout, quipped.

Morris explained the situation, so Gasaway let him throw at the end of the tryout camp so he "could return home with a clear conscience."

But Morris shocked the scouts when his fastball was clocked at ninety-eight mph. That is Nolan Ryan speed, and much faster than Morris had ever thrown during his six years in the minors more than a decade earlier.

"I think there were six catchers there that day, and we rotated around," Hardin recalled. "I remember there was this 'old guy' there, and he was the last one to pitch. I was the next catcher up, so I got behind the plate.

"He threw the first one over my head. In fact, I didn't catch the first two. I can't imagine trying to hit it. I could barely catch it. I had the biggest eyes in the world. I don't know how many fastballs he threw in a row, but they were all about ninety-eight mph. I could hear everyone talking behind me and checking their (radar) guns. Then he threw a curve and it hit me in the shoulder. I think it was bruised for two weeks. When we got done, he said he appreciated me catching him. I was in awe."

Hardin said he returned home, telling everyone in De Leon about catching "some guy who threw ninety-eight mph." But Hardin admitted he left the tryout camp not knowing if the Devil Rays had signed Morris.

They did, and Morris pitched at the Double-A and Triple-A level before being called up in mid-September as the oldest major league rookie in forty years. Morris made his first big league appearance on September 17, 1999, against the Texas Rangers at The Ballpark in Arlington.

"It was an awesome time," Morris said of major league debut. "My whole life had been up and down until that point. I hadn't seen my family in three months, and there we were in Texas. My family and kids were there. To achieve a dream I'd had since I was a kid was incredible."

Morris was called out of the bullpen with two outs in the bottom of the eighth inning to face Texas shortstop Royce Clayton. Interestingly, that was a match-up of a twenty-nine-year-old veteran of eight major-league seasons batting against a thirty-five-year-old rookie. Morris struck him out on four pitches.

"I was watching on TV that night," Hardin said. "I remember thinking I can't believe this is the guy I caught who is now pitching in the big leagues."

Morris made twenty-five relief appearances over the rest of that season and the first month of the 2000 season before re-injuring his elbow, ending his major league career.

So how was a thirty-five-year-old, who had been out of base-ball for ten years, able to throw ninty-eight mph after five surgeries on his elbow and shoulder?

"Everyone wants to know why," said Morris, who now tells his story as a motivational speaker. "I don't know. I guess the first time round, God didn't want me to do it. Ten years off let my body mature and rest."

Hardin said none of the pitchers he caught at Tarleton State threw much over ninety mph. Is there a difference between a ninety-mph fastball and a ninety-eight-mph fastball?

"There is some serious difference between ninety and ninety-eight mph," he responded emphatically.

Hardin knows. He has first-hand experience as the "first" catcher of baseball's oldest rookie.

Clair Bee and Chip Hilton

When Ronald Ross won the Chip Hilton Award in 2005, the Texas Tech senior guard admitted he had no idea who Chip Hilton was.

And no wonder. Chip Hilton was a fictional character created more than fifty years earlier by author Clair Bee.

The influence of Bee, a Hall of Fame basketball coach in addition to being the author of twenty-four books in the Chip Hilton sports series, is still being felt in the basketball world, however. And now, thanks to a Lubbock connection, Chip

Cindy and Randy Farley.

Hilton is reaching a new generation of young readers.

Randy Farley, associate director/media relations for Texas Tech men's basketball, is Bee's son-in-law. He and his wife Cindy, an English teacher at Hutchinson Junior High in Lubbock, re-released the Chip Hilton series in 1999, completing a fifteen-year effort to fulfill a promise made to Cindy's father in the final year of his life.

Since then, nearly a million "new" Chip Hilton books have been sold.

So who was Clair Bee?

Enshrined in the Naismith Memorial Basketball Hall of Fame in 1968, Bee compiled an .826 lifetime winning percentage, winning 410 games and losing only 86 from 1929-1951 at Rider College and Long Island University. That's still the best winning percentage in major-college coaching history.

Known as an innovator, Bee is credited with inventing the 1-3-1 zone defense and the three-seconds-in-the-lane rule. He is believed to be the first to conduct sports camps in the summer.

Bee also spent three years (1952-1955) as a coach and co-owner of the Baltimore Bullets in the National Basketball Association. During that time, he helped create the twenty-four-second shot clock that the NBA still uses today.

Farley said Bee was working as athletic director of the New York Military Academy in Cornwall, in the early 1960s after his coaching career was over. He was good friends with Tates Locke, the basketball coach at West Point at the time. One day, Locke introduced Bee to his new assistant coach, Bob Knight.

Knight, who had read the Chip Hilton books as a youngster himself, immediately became close friends with Bee.

"They became like father and son," Cindy said of the relationship between her father and Knight. "No one was ever more loyal to my dad than Bob Knight. Coach Knight even took him to the Hall of Fame induction ceremony one year. When I was growing up, I can remember the phone ringing after a game, and it would be Coach Knight. But he only called to discuss losses. He never called after a win."

Cindy said it was especially meaningful to her that Knight, Bee's close friend, became the winningest coach in college basketball history since her dad owns the best winning percentage of all time.

Bee wrote his first book *Touchdown Pass* in the Chip Hilton series in 1948. He penned twenty-three more over the next twenty years in what is considered the top sports fiction series ever written.

"Once, when my dad was coaching, he went to Cuba to do a basketball clinic," Cindy said, "and he met (Ernest) Hemingway. He told Hemingway that he wanted to write and wanted to know if he should go back to school and take some writing classes. Hemingway said no.

"Write about what you know and write every day," Hemingway told Bee. "If you have something to say that is real and honest, people will read it."

Bee took his first book, a novel, to publishers Grosset & Dunlap in New York.

"They turned it down but told him they'd like to turn it into a series for kids," Cindy said.

Thus, the Chip Hilton series was born, selling more than two million copies over twenty years.

"It never had huge readership, but it always had a loyal readership," Cindy said.

Bee, who became blind from glaucoma in the final years of his life, lived with the Farleys in Cleveland before his death in 1983 at age eighty-seven.

"A short time before Dad died, our son Michael, who was four or five at the time, would read the Chip Hilton books to Dad," Cindy said.

"One day when Michael finished reading to him, Coach Bee said 'those were really good,'" Randy recalled. "I told him Cindy and I will get those re-issued. When Cindy got home, I told her what I had promised."

"How are we going to do that?" Cindy asked.

"I don't have a clue," Randy replied.

The Farleys spent more than ten years searching for a publisher until an agent in Dallas hooked them up with publishers Broadman and Holman in Nashville, Tennessee. The publisher liked the idea but said the books were too outdated and needed editing in terminology.

"We decided we couldn't let someone else do that," Cindy said. "It was a huge commitment. It took four years of our life, every weekend and evening. But we each brought a love for the project. We put the books in contemporary times. Chip's mother now drives a car. Chip has a computer and watches ESPN. But it

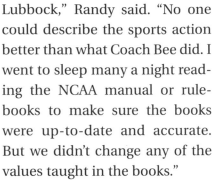

A sampling of Chip Hilton books. Courtesy of Randy and Cindy Farley.

has the same values of teamwork, family, and doing things right as the original books."

"We finished just before we moved to Lubbock," Randy said. "No one could describe the sports action better than what Coach Bee did. I went to sleep many a night reading the NCAA manual or rulebooks to make sure the books were up-to-date and accurate. But we didn't change any of the values taught in the books."

The Farley also released *Fiery Fullback*, the twenty-fourth book in the series. Bee had kept the manuscript of his final book locked away, saying America had changed too much in the turbulent 1960s to accept the wholesome values taught in the book.

With the help of Knight, the Farleys, in conjunction with the Basketball Hall of Fame, also established the Coach Clair Bee Award and the Chip Hilton Award twelve years ago. Knight won the coaching award in 2002 for his revitalization of the Texas Tech basketball program. Wake Forest's Tim Duncan, now the star for the San Antonio Spurs, was the first recipient of the Chip Hilton award, an honor given during the Final Four for a senior men's basketball player demonstrating outstanding character, leadership, and talent similar to the qualities evident in the Chip Hilton series.

Ronald Ross, who went from walk-on to team captain of an unheralded Red Raiders team that advanced to the "Sweet 16" of the NCAA Tournament, was an overwhelming choice for the award in 2005.

Farley admits that many have probably forgotten Bee, although "the students of the game would recognize his name."

But now, thanks to a promise Randy and Cindy Farley made twenty-five years ago, a new generation of youngsters has the opportunity to read about Chip Hilton and the positive influence that sports can have on their lives.

Danny Heep:
Eyewitness to History

San Antonio native Danny Heep is a footnote in baseball history. More remarkably, he was an eyewitness to two of the most memorable plays in World Series history.

Heep, now the head baseball coach at Incarnate Word University in his hometown, enjoyed an eleven-year major league career with the Houston Astros, New York Mets, Los Angeles Dodgers, and Boston Red Sox. His name is still in the record books when he clubbed four home runs as a pinch-hitter for the Mets during the 1983 season.

He also "earned" another footnote in baseball history on July 11, 1985, when Heep became Hall of Fame hurler Nolan Ryan's 4,000th career strikeout victim. Heep ran into Ryan, a fellow Texan, a couple of years later.

"I wish you'd hurry up and get to 5,000," Heep told Ryan. "I'm getting tired of people asking me about being No. 4,000."

"I'll get to 5,000," Ryan replied, with a smile, "but you'll always be No. 4,000."

Fortunately for Heep, it didn't take Ryan long to make it to 5,000, reaching that mark when he struck out Oakland outfielder Rickey Henderson on August 22, 1989. Ryan ended his career in 1993 when 5,714 career strikeouts, a mark many baseball experts believe will never be equaled.

There was much more to Heep's baseball career, however, than just being a milestone "K" among the 1,176 different players that Ryan fanned in his career. Heep, who had a .259 career batting average as an outfielder and pinch-hitter, also owns two World Series rings.

Ask any baseball fan to name the most memorable plays in World Series history, and Don Larsen's perfect game in 1956, Bill Mazerowski's walk-off ninth-inning homer in Game Seven in 1960, Boston first baseman Bill Buckner's error in Game Six in 1986, and Kirk Gibson's pinch-hit homer in Game One in 1988 are sure to make the list.

Heep was sitting in the winning dugout for both Buckner's error and Gibson's pinch-hit homer.

Boston Red Sox fans, who thought their team was cursed after failing to win a World

Coach Danny Heep tries to reason with an umpire. Courtesy of the University of the Incarnate Word.

Series since trading Babe Ruth to the New York Yankees after the 1919 season, were convinced of it after the 1986 World Series. The Red Sox led the Mets three games to two and held a 5-3 lead going into the bottom of the ninth inning in Game Six. If Boston could get three outs, the Red Sox would claim their first World Series title since 1918.

But the Mets bunched three singles and a wild pitch before Buckner let a grounder that would have been the third out roll between his legs, allowing the Mets to score the winning run in a 6-5 triumph. New York then rallied from a 3-0 deficit in Game 7 for an 8-5 victory to capture Game 7 and claim the World Series title.

For Boston fans, the "Curse of the Bambino" continued for twenty-eight more years before the Red Sox finally won the World Series in 2004.

"That first World Series in 1986 with the Mets was a lot of fun," Heep said. "It was a fun year for me. It was a young team, and it was all about team. We were all about the same age, and we were all good friends. That's something that doesn't happen very often. You have teams that have prima donnas, and teams that have personalities. But that team was committed to one thing, and that was winning. It didn't matter how much you made. It didn't matter if you were a rookie. It didn't matter if you were thirty-five years old or if you were twenty-three years old. Everybody got along. It was a fun season. I loved playing in New York. We all kind of came up together after I was traded from Houston. We went from losing 100 games to winning 116 games in a four-year span. That was fun to be a part of that turnaround."

Two years later, Heep was playing again in the World Series, this time for the Los Angeles Dodgers.

"That Oakland team was supposed to sweep us," Heep said. "That's what all the papers said. They even had some fans there that had the brooms out, and this was Game One. It wasn't like they had already won a couple. This was Game One."

Kirk Gibson was not in the Dodgers' lineup because of a hamstring injury, but Los Angeles manager Tommy Lasorda called on Gibson to pinch-hit with two outs in the bottom of the ninth inning.

"We had to help him out of the dugout, just to get up the steps," Heep recalled. "He limped up there and took a couple of weird swings. We knew he was hurting. He just sat on one pitch, which was a slider, middle out. As strong as he is, he one-handed that pitch out of the ballpark. It was amazing."

Gibson's two-out, two-strike, two-run pinch home run off Oakland relief ace Dennis Eckersley gave the Dodgers a dramatic 5-4 victory in Game One, and Los Angeles went on to win the Series four games to one over the heavily favored Athletics. It was Gibson's only plate appearance of the 1988 World Series.

Heep, first called up to the big leagues by the Astros in 1979, was traded to the Mets for pitcher Mike Scott after the 1982 season, a trade that proved to be beneficial for both teams. Heep knows how fortunate he was to play for two World Series champions.

"Great players like Ernie Banks never had a chance to do that," Heep said. "A lot of it is luck, to be in the right place at the right time and being with an organization that is committed to winning. Some organizations are, and some aren't. Some organizations are satisfied to be middle of the road. That's why everybody wants to go to the Yankees or to Boston, because they want to win a world championship. I know money has a lot to do with it, but when it gets down to brass tacks, everyone wants to have a World Series ring."

Heep has two—and an eyewitness view of two of the most memorable plays in World Series history.

Déjà vu at Augusta National

Only seven native Texans have claimed the green jacket that goes to the winner of the Masters at Augusta National Golf Club.

Byron Nelson, Ralph Gudahl, Jimmy Demaret, Ben Hogan, Jack Burke, Jr., Ben Crenshaw, and Charles Coody have combined to win

Charles Coody won the Masters in 1971. Courtesy of the Diamondback Charity Classic.

a total twelve Masters championships. But only Crenshaw (1984 and 1995) and Coody (1971) have managed to earn the coveted prize in the last fifty years.

Coody, who grew up in the small West Texas town of Stamford and now calls Abilene home, finished in the top sixty on the PGA Tour money list for thirteen consecutive years, but he won only three times during his career on the regular PGA Tour. One of those victories, however, came at the famed Bobby Jones course in Augusta, Georgia. It was a victory that Coody readily admits changed his life.

But what even avid golf fans might not know is that he also was in position to possibly win the Masters in 1969. That failed experience played a major role in the title that Coody did capture two years later.

Coody acknowledged he experienced "déjà vu" when he stepped on the tee box at the par-three sixteenth hole in the final round in 1971.

"It was unreal," he recalled. "We've all had times in our lives when we say I've done this before, I've been here before, or this is almost like a dream of something that has happened previously. When I walked up on the tee in 1969, I was firmly committed in my mind that I was going to hit a six-iron.

"I was playing with George Knudson, who had the honor on the tee. I've never hit out of anyone else's bag, but somehow, without trying to, I noticed that George hit a four-iron. The type of shot he hit was high, landed on the bank and rolled down to the lower level. That was fine except he was going to have a putt that had five or six feet of break in it. I would rather be deeper in the green and be putting uphill. It put just enough doubt in my mind that I hit a five-iron. I hit a bad shot, and we all know I didn't win the Masters in 1969."

Coody finished in a tie for fifth place with Don January at 283, two strokes behind 1969 champion George Archer. Knudson, Billy Casper and Tom Weiskopf tied for second, a stroke behind Archer and one shot in front of Coody and January.

Two years later, Coody again stood on the sixteenth tee at Augusta National with a chance to win the prestigious tournament.

"When I walked up there on Sunday in 1971, it was so eerie," he said. "The shadows were the same. It was the same time of day. The pin was in the same place. I had the same yardage. It was unbelievable. Everything was the same. I had to make sure I slowed myself down and didn't just grab the six-iron and hit too quick because I had the honors. Fortunately this time, I hit a good shot, about ten feet behind the hole and I made the putt (for his second straight birdie)."

Coody then closed out the round with back-to-back pars on seventeen and eighteen to clinch the championship with a nine-under par 279 total.

"(Johnny) Miller was in the process of bogeying eighteen, although I didn't know that at the time," Coody said. "At that point, as far as I knew, I had a two-shot lead over Jack (Nicklaus) who was playing behind me and a one-shot lead on Miller. He bogeyed eighteen, and Jack parred in, so I won by two strokes."

Coody said trying to hold off Nicklaus in 1971 could probably be compared to most PGA Tour golfers today trying to hang on to a lead with Tiger Woods nipping at their heels.

"If you would have asked any patron who came in the gate that day, who they expected to win the tournament, they would have said Jack," Coody said. "If you would have asked me—if I was being 100 percent honest—I would have probably said Jack, too. But all I knew was that I was going to go out there and try to play as good a round as I knew how to play under those circumstances and not be concerned about what Jack was doing because I had no control over what Jack did."

The green jacket now hangs in a trophy case in Coody's Abilene home. How did that victory change his life?

"Well, it gave me lifetime recognition with the golfing public, the average spectator," he said. "A guy can win fifteen tournaments—which is a fabulous career—but not win a major, and only the avid golfer can tell you what tournaments he won. But everyone can tell you that Charles Coody, George Archer, Tommy Aaron, Gay Brewer and Bob Goalby won the Masters, even though they aren't Jack Nicklaus or Arnold Palmer. It is lifetime recognition, and I still make money out of it today. I did several corporate dinners this year at Augusta that I have no doubt I would not have done if I hadn't won the Masters."

At age sixty-eight, thirty-five years after his Masters victory, Coody found the magic one last time among the blooming dogwoods and azaleas. He had told the Masters committee prior to the 2006 tournament that it would be his final competitive rounds at Augusta National.

After opening with an eighty-nine—a round which Coody said "embarrassed myself"—he fired a stellar two-over-par seventy-four on Friday in his final official eighteen holes at the Masters.

With his son Kyle carrying his bag, Coody made birdies at Nos. 3, 4, 12 and 15 and was one-under par as he approached the sixteenth tee box, the site of the pivotal moment of his career. Coody was on the verge of becoming the first golfer over the age of sixty to break par at the Masters.

"I had birdied fifteen to go one under for the round," he said. "In reflection, I got a little ahead of myself. I got to thinking about how nice it would be to do that rather than doing it and thinking how nice it was. As the young guys say today, I guess I lost my focus a little bit. I bogeyed sixteen, and on seventeen I hit a bad tee shot and wound up with a double bogey."

Coody then parred eighteen to finish with a two-over-par seventy-four, a score that beat thirty-six other "younger" players that day. For one last time, Coody heard the cheers echo for him around the hallowed Georgia hills. The reporters wanted to talk to him after his round, and his story was featured on ESPN's "SportsCenter." It was a fitting climax to a career that has been so intertwined with the golf's most prestigious event.

"If someone would have told me before I teed off on the first hole that I would shoot a seventy-four today," he said, "I would have said 'just mark it down and let's go have a cup of coffee.'"

Football's Most Unusual Play

R ice University's Dicky Maegle (then known as Moegle) had one of the greatest games in college football bowl history on January, 1, 1954, when he set a bowl record with 265 yards rushing and scored on touchdown runs of seventy-nine, ninety-five and thirty-four yards. He averaged an incredible twenty-four yards per play on just eleven carries as Rice defeated Alabama 28-6 at the Cotton Bowl.

But no one remembers Maegle's performance that day. Instead, his name is forever linked to Alabama's Tommy Lewis in college football's most unusual play.

Here is what happened on that New Year's Day in Dallas:

The Crimson Tide had grabbed an early 6-0 lead on Lewis' one-yard run, but Moegle raced seventy-nine yards—at the time a new Cotton Bowl record—in the opening seconds of the second quarter to put Rice in front 7-6.

Minutes later, Alabama moved back into scoring position but fumbled the ball away at the Owls' ten-yard line. On the first play from scrimmage, Rice was penalized five yards for illegal procedure. Facing first-and-fifteen from the five-yard line, what followed turned out to be a play of historical proportions.

Maegle took a handoff from Rice quarterback Leroy Fenstemaker and swept right end. The Owls blocked the play perfectly as described in the Cotton Bowl Classic's record book:

"Blois Bridges made the block to help Maegle turn the corner. Mac Taylor flattened another Alabama defender, and Gordon Kellog took out the last man—Bart Starr, the future Green Bay

Packers quarterback who was playing left defensive halfback for the Crimson Tide—and Maegle was long gone.

"As Maegle approached midfield in front of the Alabama bench, Lewis leaped off the bench, stepped around a couple of teammates, ran laterally down the sideline before throwing a perfect block into Maegle's blind side as he hit the forty-two-yard mark. As some 75,000 fans looked on in disbelief, game announcers fumbled for words to describe what had just taken place. Maegle lay motionless on the turf. Referee Cliff Shaw, who had been following the play up the field, hesitated for a moment and then shot his arms over his head, signaling touchdown."

Sportswriters covering the game were reportedly divided over whether Maegle would have scored on the play, although Maegle had teammate Dick Chapman nearby to screen Bill Oliver, the only Alabama player who appeared to have a shot at making a touchdown-saving tackle.

Nearly a year later, writers participating in an Associated Press year-end poll voted the ninety-five-yard play as the sports oddity in 1954. It remains, with an asterisk, the longest—and most talked about—play in Cotton Bowl history.

Indeed, more than a half-century later, it remains as perhaps the most unusual play in college football history.

From Sitting to Coaching Legend

Fans always enjoy the "Where Are They Now" features in newspapers and magazines, allowing readers to catch up on a former star athlete who is no longer in the limelight. *Sports Illustrated* offers an interesting "Where Are They Now" feature in its magazine each week.

In thirty years of covering youth and high school sports, I remain fascinated by the "Look At What They Have Become" aspect of sports. Unfortunately, we don't have a crystal ball to look into the future to determine what student-athletes will become in the future.

But it is interesting to look back at a particular game and realize what happened to some of those youthful participants.

I still remember one of my reporters coming back to the office from an American Junior Golf Association tournament at Fairway Oaks Country Club in Abilene in 1987.

"Who won? I asked.

"Some left-handed sixteen-year-old kid from San Diego named Phil Mickelson," he replied.

Wonder whatever became of him?

In covering Class 5A high school football, the state's largest classification, the "Look At What They Have Become" aspect happens quite often. In the 1996 Class 5A Division II state championship game at Texas Stadium that I covered, Drew Brees led Austin Westlake to a victory over Abilene Cooper and Dominic Rhodes. Brees is now the quarterback of the New Orleans Saints and Rhodes rushed for 113 yards and a touchdown in the Indianapolis Colts' victory in Super Bowl XLI.

Even a local regular-season football game can feature future stars. The showdown in Abilene between Abilene High and Abilene Cooper annually attracts 16,000 fans to a jam-packed Shotwell Stadium. Who could have guessed the future of four players in the 1995 crosstown rivalry?

John Lackey and Ahmad Brooks were splitting time at quarterback for Abilene High that season. Lackey went on to win Game Seven of the World Series for the Los Angeles Angels in 2002 and is now one of the top pitchers in the American League. Brooks became a three-year starter at defensive back for the Texas Longhorns and played one year for the Buffalo Bills in the National Football League.

Cooper teammates Justin Snow and Dominic Rhodes became the first high school teammates to be members of a winning Super Bowl team in 2007. Stories like these can be told over and over with the talent of Texas high school football.

Obviously, it doesn't occur nearly as often in the smaller classifications. But it does happen. In 1973, Big Sandy, a small school near Longview in East Texas, defeated Rule, a tiny school sixty miles northwest of Abilene, in the Class B state championship game. The starting quarterback for Rule that day was Art Briles, now the head football coach at the University of Houston. Starting at linebacker for Big Sandy was Lovie Smith, now the head coach of the Chicago Bears.

But what is equally as fascinating is who *wasn't* playing that day. Wes Kittley, the hugely successful track coach at Texas Tech, was a freshman at Rule in the fall of 1973, but he wasn't allowed to play football.

"I loved football," Kittley recalled. "I was the quarterback on our seventh grade team. But then I got hit in the head with a basketball."

Kittley suffered a detached retina, and doctors insisted no more contact sports. In fact, Kittley had to stay home as an eighth grader.

"I was home-schooled with Art's mother," Kittley said. "Wanda Briles came to our house and tutored me that year."

With football and basketball ruled out, Kittley turned his attention to track when he returned to school as a freshman. He is one of four Kittley brothers to win a gold medal at the state track meet.

In the spring of 1974, the Class B state track meet appeared to be a rematch of the state football title game the previous fall. The team championship came down to the final event, the mile relay. If Big Sandy won the race, it would be state champion. If Rule captured the event, the Bobcats would be state champs.

"I ran third," Kittley said. "My brother Rob handed off to me, and I handed off to Art."

Rule won the mile relay, claiming the state team championship and exacting a small measure of revenge against Big Sandy.

Kittley became a three-time all-American in the 800 meters at Abilene Christian University. He took over as the women's track coach at ACU in 1985 and then added the men's program to his duties in 1993.

He won an unprecedented twenty-nine NCAA Division II track championships during his tenure at ACU. In 1996, he became the first coach to win the men's and women's indoor and outdoor national track championships in the same year. He won all four again in 1999. No other coach has ever achieved that feat. He has been inducted in to the ACU, Big Country, and Lone Star Conference halls of fame.

In 2000, Texas Tech lured Kittley away from his alma mater to rebuild its sagging track program. Just five short years later, Kittley led the Red Raiders to the school's first Big 12 men's track championship.

"That was the hardest thing I've ever done professionally," Kittley said of turning around the downtrodden Tech track program. "We were last in the conference, only scoring twelve points at the conference meet. We had to start from scratch. It was a building process to get numbers and quality."

His team had four individual champions at the 2005 Big 12 meet, led by Olympian Jonathan Johnson. After the successful conference meet, Kittley took thirty-one of his athletes, the most out of any program in the country, to Sacramento for the 2005 Outdoor National Championships. The Red Raiders brought ten All-American awards back to Lubbock.

Texas Tech track Coach Wes Kittley won twenty-nine national championships at Abilene Christian before taking over at Tech. Courtesy Abilene Christian University.

Briles and Smith are just two amazing success stories from the Class B state football championship game in 1973. An errant basketball kept Kittley from being on the field that December afternoon, too, but it certainly hasn't hampered his own remarkable coaching career. Look at what those three small-town kids have become.

Instant Replay

Upon further review...

Football fans have been hearing those words during National Football League games for a number of years. But instant replay came to college football for the first time in 2005.

Although it proved to be a success and played a prominent role in a number of college games, instant replay's most visible impact came in the 2005 regular-season finale between Oklahoma and Texas Tech at Jones-SBC Stadium in Lubbock.

Here was the situation:

Trailing 21-17, Texas Tech took possession at its own thirty-five-yard-line with 1:33 remaining and no timeouts. Cody Hodges completed passes of twenty-six and seven yards to Robert Johnson and an eighteen-yarder to Danny Amendola to help get the Red Raiders to the Oklahoma five-yard line with thirteen seconds remaining.

Instant replay was used to uphold Amendola's fourth-down catch in which he and an OU defender came down with the ball simultaneously, the first of three times that plays were reviewed on the thirteen-play drive.

Hodges then threw an apparent TD pass to Joe Filani, but instant replay reversed the call, claiming Filani was still bobbling the ball when he went out of bounds.

So, after two instant replays—one that went Tech's way and one that was ruled in the Sooners' favor—the game came down to one last play, fourth down at the two-yard line with two seconds to play. A trip to the Cotton Bowl was riding on the outcome for the Red Raiders.

Tech coach Mike Leach shocked everyone by calling a running play, a handoff up the middle to senior running back Taurean Henderson.

"They were playing man coverage," Hodges explained after the game. "And if you look at it, Oklahoma had exactly 11 guys on the line of scrimmage and we have talked about it, as a running back all they have to do is break a little bubble and there is nobody behind that front line to stop him. Coach Leach, on that last play, said if you have to, throw it, but if you think Taurean can run in there, then do it. I just feel like if you have Taurean in there and he has three yards and is running downhill as fast as possible, regardless of how far he has to go, I think he has got a good chance."

But did Henderson get into the end zone?

The play was reviewed but the touchdown call was upheld. On television replays, multiple camera angles from the near side and one from behind and above the end zone seemed inconclusive. It appeared that Henderson rolled across the leg of one of the Oklahoma defenders laying on the ground. There were no camera angles from the far side of the field, where the official who made the TD call was positioned.

"I was very confident that I had got to the line of scrimmage," Henderson said. "But you never know, because at any time they could change it. So, I was a little bit nervous. I felt strongly in myself that I had scored."

After the lengthy delay that finally resulted with the touchdown call, stadium officials took down the goalposts to prevent fans from ripping them down. But this bizarre game wasn't quite over yet even though no time remained on the clock. The game officials made them raise the posts back up for the extra-point try because if Oklahoma blocked the extra point, the Sooners could return it the length of the field for a game-tying two-point safety.

Tech snapped the ball but never attempted the kick, instead purposely downing the ball and thus ending the game.

After the game, the two coaches almost sounded like they were on the other's team. OU's Bob Stoops didn't dispute the game-winning call on Henderson's run.

"I didn't see it and I'm not going to sit here and criticize," he said. "We have a system in place and you hope that it works and it makes the calls that are correct."

Leach, however, was left wondering about the validity of using instant replay.

"I'm starting to rethink my position on instant replays," he said. "There is no dialogue at that point. The review happens and the decision is made. I felt like we scored twice. There was a lot of time between plays. I have mixed feelings about it. We are not much better off with it. Things are still even. I wonder if it is worth the time that goes into it."

Has there ever been a more unusual finish? Texas Tech knocked off Oklahoma 23-21 in a game that featured three instant replays from inside the five-yard line in the last thirteen seconds and finally ended with the winning team intentionally missing the extra point.

Upon further review, the Red Raiders and Sooners in 2005 staged one the most unusual thrillers in college football history.

The One Man Gang
From Bangs

··

James Segrest had a remarkable career in track and field.

As an athlete, he teamed with three-time Olympic gold medalist Bobby Morrow, Waymon Griggs and Bill Woodhouse to set five world records in the 440- and 880-yard relays during his collegiate years at Abilene Christian University from 1956-1958. He was a member of ACU's NAIA national championship team in 1955 and finished sixth in the NCAA Division I 200 meters in 1956. During his four years at Abilene Christian, the Wildcats had a record of 52-9 in the 440 and 880 relays, and Segrest ran in all 61 races. His personal best times were 9.7 in the 100 yards, 20.7 for the 220 and 47.7 for the 440.

As a track coach, Segrest won a state championship at Monahans and captured eleven National Junior College Athletic Association indoor and outdoor national track titles at Odessa College. He also was the head coach for the U.S. team at the World University Games in Mexico City in 1979.

But Segrest, who is now retired and lives in Granbury, is best remembered for a nickname he earned in high school: "The One Man Gang From Bangs." He doesn't even know who is responsible for giving him that moniker.

"It may have been a sports writer in Brownwood," he said. "But to be honest, I don't know for sure. It first appeared in the papers the Sunday after the state track meet."

And the name stuck.

Segrest grew up in Bangs, a small town just ten miles west of Brownwood. He was Bangs' only entrant in the 1954 Class A track and field state championship meet in Austin, but he became an instant Texas high school legend for his performance.

Segrest won the 100, 220 and 440 and placed fourth in the long jump to score 34 points by himself to single-handedly win the state championship for the Bangs Dragons. Thus, the nickname "The One Man Gang From Bangs" was born.

"I remember the public address announcer at Memorial Stadium announced that Bangs had won the team championship and asked the Bangs team report to the victory stand," Segrest recalled. "When just my coach and I went up there, Dr. Ray Williams (then the executive director of the University Interscholastic League) asked, 'Where is the rest of your team.' My coach said, 'Well, you had just one track meet, didn't you?'"

Segrest's performance remains the only time in the state track and field meet history that one athlete has single-handedly captured a team championship.

Among the other highlights of his remarkable career is Segrest's involvement in a dual track meet with the Soviet Union.

Segrest, along with other such legendary track stars as Rafer Johnson and Parry O'Brien, was a member of the first U.S. national team to compete against the Soviet Union in a dual meet at Lenin Stadium in Moscow in 1958.

"It was during the Cold War," Segrest remembered. "Russia was so far behind us in clothing and everything else. It was altogether different. We stayed in the Leningrad Hotel, and we had straw mattresses. We couldn't drink the water because it came right out of the Moscow River. When we left our hotel, the Russian people would flock to us. They wanted to buy our Levis."

Despite all of his many successes, Segrest was introduced at both Texas Sports Hall of Fame and Big Country Athletic Hall of Fame induction banquets as "The One Man Gang from Bangs."

Some unknown sports writer somewhere certainly coined a winning nickname that is still remembered today, fifty-three years after Segrest's remarkable one-day performance at the state high school track meet in Austin.

Finding Gems in Small Towns

Having grown up myself in a small town that was one stop-light short of a having one stoplight, I admit I enjoy seeing small-town kids achieve success.

For example, much was made of Colt McCoy's hometown at the start of the 2006 football season as the redshirt freshman was tabbed to replace Vince Young as the quarterback of the defending national champion Texas Longhorns.

McCoy, whose name Colt only seemed to help further his small-town legend, grew up in tiny Tuscola, population 714. ABC-TV even pin-pointed Tuscola on a Texas map during its telecast of the early-season match-up featuring No. 1 Ohio State against No. 2

Texas quarterback Colt McCoy. Courtesy of Doug Holleman/Texas Football.

Texas. McCoy played at Jim Ned High School where he became the all-time leading passer in Texas Class 2A football history.

"Art Briles (University of Houston head coach) was here the other day," Colt's father and coach Brad McCoy said during the recruiting progress in the spring of 2004. "He said Colt has to be good for everyone to come here, because no one goes through Tuscola."

As the coaches from the nation's top college football programs first began recruiting McCoy, the first thing they discovered is they couldn't find Jim Ned on a Texas map. That's because it doesn't exist. It is the name for a consolidated school district that includes five small towns in south Taylor County in West Texas. The district's high school is located in Tuscola, eighteen miles south of Abilene.

"I had more than one coach call and say he couldn't find Jim Ned on a map," said Brad McCoy, now the head football coach at Graham, another small West Texas town. "Then I had to tell everyone who Jim Ned was."

Jim Ned was an Indian scout for the cavalry that patrolled the West Texas frontier in the mid-1800s. He gave his name to Jim Ned Creek, which, in turn, prompted the name for the school district.

"My family wants me to stay in Texas," Colt McCoy said when he made his commitment to the Longhorns and Texas coach Mack Brown. "I'm born and raised in Texas and plan to stay in Texas. If you're going to stay in Texas, UT is the place to be."

The small-town legend of Colt grew in 2006 as McCoy was named the Big 12 Conference Offensive Freshman of the Year. He appeared on the cover of the 2007 issue of Dave Campbell's *Texas Football* magazine, trumpeting his small-town roots and big-time success.

While becoming a star—especially a quarterback—at a major college like the University of Texas after growing up in a small town is indeed rare, it has happened before. In fact, four of the seven most recent inductees into the Texas Tech Athletic Hall of Honor grew up in small West Texas towns.

The Class of 2006 Hall of Honor at Texas Tech was headlined by Miami Dolphins linebacker Zach Thomas, who grew up in tiny White Deer in the Texas Panhandle before moving to Pampa in high school.

But three other members of the Class of 2006 were small-town athletes who were unheralded and could easily have been overlooked. Instead, Michi Atkins of Loraine, Don Rives of Wheeler and Harold Hudgens of Ballinger went on to make their mark at Texas Tech.

Rives believes he received an opportunity in the early 1970s that might not be available to a similar small-town athlete today.

"I would have never been recruited today," he said. "They could sign fifty players every year back then, so they could venture down into Class A and 2A."

Rives became a key defensive player at nose guard from 1970-1972 during the early teams of the Jim Carlen era at Tech. He was named second-team all-American and consensus all-Southwest Conference in 1972 and followed his senior year with appearance in the Coaches All-America game and the Hula Bowl. He was named to the SWC all-decade team of the 1970s and in 1990 was named to the All-Time Texas Tech football team.

The late Jim Parmer, a long-time scout in Texas and the Southwest for the Chicago Bears, drafted Rives in the fifteenth round (There are only seven rounds in the National Football League draft today.). Rives made the squad and spent six years playing linebacker for the Bears alongside such notable players at Dick Butkus and Walter Payton.

Rives was named the national lineman of the week for his performance against Southern Methodist University in 1972.

"I had twenty-two or twenty-three tackles, but that guy (SMU's center) couldn't block my daughter," laughed Rives, downplaying his performance. "The big thing for me was the opportunity to play football for a kid from Wheeler."

The Red Raiders met North Carolina in the 1972 Sun Bowl, the site of one of Rives' biggest disappointments.

"I picked up a blocked punt and returned it fifty yards for a touchdown," he recalled, "but it was called back because of a penalty. They called a penalty on Coach Carlen because he was on the field. If you look back at the film, he must have been on the field two yards. The ref had to do a little jig to go around him. When you're a nose guard, you don't have many chances to score a touchdown. I wasn't very kind to the referee. We lost the game by three points."

Rives is now the head football coach at Morton, another small West Texas town.

Like Rives, Harold Hudgens was an overlooked small-town athlete who made the most of his opportunity to play at Texas Tech. He was a key player on the Red Raiders basketball teams that won back-to-back league titles in 1961 and 1962, the first Southwest Conference titles in any sport in school history.

"I was a skinny 6'8", 195-pound kid with no coordination coming out of high school (in Ballinger)," said Hudgens. "My uncle, Edgar Payne, was the basketball coach at Lubbock High, and he put a bug in Coach (Polk) Robison's ear. It was a last-minute offer. Coach Robison and Gene Gibson came down to Ballinger and worked me out. They offered me a scholarship on the spot."

Hudgens, who eventually grew to 6'10", 225 pounds, didn't make an impact until his junior season. In the 1960-1961 campaign, however, he scored thirty-one points in the season opener against Kansas in the Lubbock Coliseum that year, despite playing much of the game on what turned out to be a hairline fracture in his ankle. He missed the next eight games, and Tech lost seven of them.

But when he returned to the lineup, Hudgens averaged twenty-two points per game—the eighth-best season in school history—and led Tech to an 11-3 conference mark and its first SWC title. The Red Raiders lost to eventual national champion Cincinnati in the Midwest Regional semifinals in Kansas City, but then defeated Houston in the consolation game for the school's first NCAA tournament victory. Hudgens was the leading scorer in the regional tournament.

The Red Raiders tied SMU for the 1962 SWC title and then defeated the Mustangs in a one-game playoff to earn a second consecutive trip to the NCAA Tournament. Tech beat the Air Force Academy to advance to the Midwest Regional, but Creighton and Colorado State defeated the Raiders in the regional tournament.

Hudgens was a unanimous all-SWC selection and earned all-America honors from *Look* magazine and the Helms Foundation.

"The biggest highlight was we brought Tech into the forefront of the Southwest Conference," he said.

Hudgens still lives in his hometown of Ballinger and is the chief financial offer of the Northern Runnels County Hospital Association in Winters.

No one came from a smaller town than Michi Atkins, however. In fact, some may have questioned what Marsha Sharp was thinking when she recruited Atkins out of tiny Loraine, a school so small it plays six-man football and had little girls' basketball tradition.

But Atkins made her mark immediately as a freshman when she was a key contributor for the 1993 national champion Lady Raider basketball team. She downplayed the transition from such a small school to being a member of the collegiate national championship team.

Michi Atkins of tiny Loraine became an All-American at Texas Tech. Courtesy of Texas Tech sports information office.

"I didn't have a choice in the matter," Atkins stated. "I remember blocking a couple of Sheryl Swoopes' shots in practice and thinking, 'Wow, she's the best player there is.' Coach Sharp told me to put my jersey on with the 'red' on the outside, and I never looked back. It wasn't that difficult."

Atkins was named all-SWC each of the next three years and was twice selected the Southwest Conference Player of the

Year. By the time she left Texas Tech, she had scored 2,134 points and grabbed 927 rebounds, both third-best totals in school history.

When asked to name a highlight of her career, Atkins responded, "Aside from winning the national championship, beating the Lady Longhorns on their home court for the first time (during her freshman season) was the most exhilarating."

She finished her career as the all-time leading scorer in Southwest Conference women's basketball history.

"That still amazes me," she said, "playing behind players like Carolyn Thompson and Sheryl Swoopes. It was a very humbling experience what I got to go through at Texas Tech."

Atkins, a mother of two who now lives in Fort Worth, averaged 20.9 points per game as a senior when she was named a first-team all-American.

In Texas, the stars not only come from Dallas and Houston but they also grow up in places like Tuscola, Wheeler, Ballinger and Loraine.

From Juggling Sports To Writing A Hit Song

Let's be honest. After writing more than 1,000 columns and covering high school games and interviewing high school athletes for more than thirty years, I don't remember every interview or every story.

One interview, however, that I do remember—not necessarily for the story but for the picture we took to illustrate the story—came in my first year in Texas. Clyde, a small town located just east of Abilene, had a star athlete who had earned all-state honors in football and basketball and had just qualified for the state track meet in the shot put.

"We'd like to take a picture of you holding a football, basketball and a shot," I told Elliott Park, as he met me and the *Abilene Reporter-News* photographer at the Clyde High School field house.

Clyde's Elliott Park could juggle sports before writing a hit song. Courtesy of Elliott Park.

Moments later, Park asked, "Do you want me to juggle these?" as he stood there holding all three.

"You can juggle them?" I responded, with some obvious doubt in my voice.

To my amazement, Park adeptly juggled a football, basketball and shot as our photographer shot the picture.

I continued to follow Park's athletic career as he came to McMurry University in Abilene to play basketball. Today, however, I still remember that interview for a much different reason—the success that Park has had away from athletic competition.

In the fall of 2006, he laughed when we talked again, remembering the picture taken of him juggling nearly twenty years earlier. Only this time our conversation wasn't about sports. It was about the number one song in country music that Park had written.

Park, a commercial artist and songwriter still living in his hometown, co-wrote "I Loved Her First," a ballad about a father giving his daughter away on her wedding day. The song, recorded by the group Heartland, first began receiving play on the radio on June 1, 2006. It then completed the climb to the top on October 17 when it officially hit number one on the *Radio and Record* magazine and *Billboard* magazine country music charts.

"It is a validation of everything that my wife and friends told me, that my stuff was good enough," he said at the time.

Park said the hit song was actually four years in the making.

"I came up with the idea for the song four years ago," he explained. "I had a couple of lines, the title, a little melody and the chorus. But I didn't do anything with it for nearly two years. I knew it could be a good song, and I wanted it to be a special song."

Park said he signed with a publisher, the Extreme Writers Group, in Nashville in 2003. In February 2004, Park said he went to Nashville and his publisher hooked him up with Walt Aldridge, a veteran song writer originally from Muscle Shoals, Alabama, who has had a half dozen number one hits.

"He's had a lot of success," he said of Aldridge, who co-wrote the song with Park. "He's a veteran. We met in a little writing room that had a piano in it at my publisher's office. When I was sitting in there, waiting on him, I was so nervous, but he's just a nice guy. He shook my hand and said, 'what do you have?'

"My publisher had already told me that the way this works is that the less experienced writer brings the idea to the table. So I opened my satchel and pulled out a couple of ideas. He then asked 'What else do you have?' The third idea I pitched was 'I Loved Her First.' I told him I pictured it as a waltz, but I know no one wants to record a waltz these days."

Park said he played a little of the melody on the piano for Aldridge.

"He said 'that's a great idea' and he started running with it," Park said. "He wrote of lot of the first verse, and then I jumped in and wrote the second verse. It was truly a fifty-fifty co-write. We finished it in four hours."

Park said they then invited Michael Martin to listen to it.

"He loved it," Park added. "I still have that on cassette."

It took two years and three months from that initial song-writing session to finally get the song recorded, however.

"My publisher pitched it to everybody," Park said. "They'd say they liked it but they didn't want to record it because it made them look old enough to have a daughter getting married. You know image is everything. Finally, Heartland, a new group from Alabama, came along and saw it for what it is—a good song."

It was Heartland's first single to be released nationally.

"It came out on the radio on June 1," Park said. "Within a few weeks it caught fire. It's on a little independent label, Lofton Creek. Mike Borchetta (the label owner) is from the old school. He sent out copies of the single and called DJs and said just play it and give it a chance. The phones lit up. Within a few weeks, it was the No. 1 requested song on the radio in the country. That's what is really neat. The song's success was driven by requests. That is rare these days because the major record labels spend so much money in promoting their songs."

Amazingly, "I Loved Her First" reached No. 1 on the country charts even though it is Park's first single, it was his first co-writing session and it is Heartland's first single. That is almost unheard of. The song was nominated for an ASCAP award in 2007 for its prominent air play.

Park said he has no intention of moving to Nashville.

"I have a publisher who believes in me and pushes my stuff there," he said. "I wouldn't trade any success I'd have by moving to Nashville for what I have here. This is home. I know everyone here, and my kids are close to their grandparents."

Besides, Park was living in Clyde when his first song reached No. 1 on the national country charts, juggling his business, a songwriting career, family obligations and serving on the school board. The song that became a hit often sung at weddings was written by a Texan, who obviously learned more than just the ability to juggle a football, basketball and track career in high school.

The First Interleague Hit

Here is a trivia question: Name the first Texas Ranger to bat in a postseason game.

A second trivia question: Name the first major league player to get a hit in an interleague game.

Darryl Hamilton is the answer to both questions.

After twenty-four seasons of futility, the Rangers finally won their first American League West Division title in 1996. The Rangers then faced the New York Yankees in the first round of the divisional playoffs.

Hamilton batted lead-off and played centerfield for Texas in 1996, so he was the first batter in Game One of the series at Yankee Stadium.

Hamilton had a terrific 1996 season in Arlington. He batted .293 with 184 hits and ninety-three runs in 143 games. He didn't make an error the entire season, developing a reputation of being the slickest-fielding centerfielder to ever don a Ranger uniform.

"I loved playing in this ballpark," Hamilton said of The Ballpark in Arlington, now known as Ameriquest Field.

Despite those impressive numbers, Texas opted to not re-sign the free agent. Instead, Hamilton signed with the San Francisco Giants.

But eight months later, on June 12, 1997, Hamilton was back in The Ballpark in Arlington, playing center field for the Giants against the Rangers in the first interleague game in baseball history.

Batting lead-off for San Francisco, Hamilton thus became not only the first player to bat in an interleague game but also the first to get a base hit when he lined a 2-1 pitch from Darren Oliver into right field for a single to lead off the top of the first inning.

"I hadn't thought about it," Hamilton said that night of making his mark in baseball history. "When I'm old and gray, I'll think about it. But it is interesting. It's always great to be first in anything. If interleague play stays, I'll always be first."

Interleague play has remained, proving popular for the fans and celebrating its tenth anniversary during the 2006 season.

The Giants beat the Rangers 4-3 in that first interleague game. Mark Gardner was the first winning pitcher, and Rod Beck recorded the first save. Stan Javier had the first home run and Glenallen Hill became the first National League designated hitter in a regular-season game.

Hamilton admitted he had mixed feelings about his return to the city where he enjoyed such a fantastic season a year earlier.

"It's kind of bittersweet," he said. "The organization decided to make another turn. When they first signed me (as a free agent from the Milwaukee Brewers), they said they'd take care of me if I put up the numbers. When that didn't happen, it bothered me. But that's the way the game is now. I'm lucky it worked out in San Francisco."

Hamilton, who returned to Arlington for the tenth anniversary celebration of the Rangers' first divisional championship game on August 11-12, 2006, retired from baseball in 2001 after spending thirteen seasons with the Milwaukee Brewers, Rangers, Giants, Colorado Rockies and New York Mets.

The Baton Rouge, Louisiana, native had a nice career, hitting .291 with 51 home runs and 454 RBI. But Hamilton is best remembered for his defense. On April 9, 1993, while playing for the Brewers, he set an American League record by handling his 541st consecutive chance without an error in a 6-5 win over the Oakland Athletics.

Hamilton committed only fourteen errors in his entire career as an outfielder, mostly in center field. That is an amazing statistic when one considers he handled 2,773 total chances in 1,276 games.

Indeed, those are remarkable numbers, but Hamilton will always be in the record book as the first Texas Ranger to bat in a postseason contest and the first major leaguer to bat—and get a hit—in an interleague game.

Unusual Holes-In-One

Golfers, both good and average, make holes-in-one every day. Although almost commonplace these days, every ace has a story.

According to a 2000 study conducted by Francis Scheid, Ph.D., the retired chairman of the math department at Boston University, writing for *Golf Digest* magazine, the odds of an average golfer making a hole-in-one in a given round is 12,000-to-1. Scheid figured the odds of a PGA Tour player making an ace in a given round at 3,000-to-1 and the odds of one player making two holes-in-one in the same round at 67 million-to-1.

Even 67-million-to-1 odds are possible, however. Chase Williams, a junior at Aledo High School, took fourth in the fourteen-fifteen-year-old division of the Northern Texas PGA Westcott Medalist Tour event at Hawk's Creek Golf Club in Fort Worth in June 2005, but he beat the odds that day, recording two aces in the same round.

He began his round at No. 15 because of a shotgun start, and he aced his third hole, the 120-yard No. 17 with a pitching wedge. When he reached the 190-yard No. 10 hole—Williams' fourteenth hole of the day—he drew his rescue club out of the bag and hit it in the hole.

When the ball disappeared, he said he started jumping up and down. His father Greg and grandfather Bobby were watching from the green.

"Of course, when I saw it go in, my first reaction was to look back to the tee," Greg Williams told dfwgolfnews.com. "Chase was off the ground so far, he could have dunked over Michael Jordan's head."

Sometimes holes-in-one defy even the astronomical odds that Scheid calculated. These are four such stories, tales of unusual holes-in-one by ordinary golfers in Texas. Each one received national attention.

Danny Leake, a fifty-three-year-old Lubbock insurance agent who claims a fourteen handicap, was playing in the sixth flight at the Texas Tech Rawls Course club championship during the summer of 2006.

Although he has been playing golf for thirty years, Leake recorded his first ever hole-in-one on Saturday of the tournament, acing the sixth hole with a five-iron from 174 yards out. The next day he made another hole-in-one with the same club on the same hole from 178 yards out in Sunday's final round.

"I've always wanted to make a hole-in-one, but I'm nowhere near as good a golfer as most of the people (at the tournament)," Leake told the *Lubbock Avalanche-Journal*. "That's what makes this whole thing crazy. I'll probably never hit another one as long as I live, but I'm OK with that."

Scheid didn't calculate the odds of making holes-in-one on the same hole on back-to-back days, but they have to be pretty phenomenal.

"I think he's going to get a lot of national attention for this," added Jack North, managing director of the Rawls course, in the Lubbock newspaper story. "I don't think anyone has ever hit two holes-in-one on consecutive days on the same hole, especially in a tournament. I've never even heard of such a thing."

North was right. The story of Leake's holes-in-one made national news, including a full-blown account on ESPN.com.

If holes-in-one on the same hole on back-to-back days are unheard of, then what are the odds of two holes-in-one on the same hole?

It is impossible to beat a hole-in-one in a scramble golf tournament, but one team tried during the 1992 McMurry University

Golf Classic, a four-person scramble benefiting the school's golf team. The tournament used a shotgun start, and Jason Hutt, a freshman golfer from Breckenridge, was the first to hit that morning on his team's first hole, the par-three, No. 12 hole at Abilene Country Club.

"It was playing about 150 yards from the back tee," recalled Hutt, who hit an eight-iron. "The first swing of the day. We heard it hit the stick."

The team already had a "1" marked on its scorecard, but his three teammates decided to go ahead and hit, just to "warm up," according to Hutt.

The late Garnet Gracy, a retired banker, then hit a four-iron from the front tee, which was set at 135 yards from the pin, to record the first ace of his career.

"What are the odds of that happening," Gracy said at the time. "Zilch, I think."

"The thing I remember is that it was real foggy that morning," Hutt recalled. "We didn't know for sure if Garnet's shot went in. But when we got to the green, both balls were the hole."

Hutt, now the golf coach at Cisco High School, said his ace that day was the third of his career (he hit two at Breckenridge Country Club when he was in high school). But he hasn't hit one since.

Their other two teammates, Steve Strain and Joe Burk, somehow failed to duplicate Hutt's and Gracy's efforts that day.

Anson's Hoolie White, like Leake, also made only two holes-in-one in his life, and they were on the same hole, too. But they didn't come on back-to-back days. Instead, they came more than 50 years apart.

"Kenneth (Herndon) said, 'Hurry, ball,'" White said in describing the hole-in-one he made on April 28, 1997, "and then the danged thing went in the hole."

White's hole-in-one came at the par-three, 139-yard No. 6 hole at his hometown Anson Golf Club course, located twenty-two miles northwest of Abilene. White was ninety-one years old when he sank the hole-in-one, just the second of his golfing career. But what attracted national coverage of White's ace was the fact that his only other hole-in-one came at the same hole—at least fifty years earlier.

White, who had been playing the nine-hole Anson Golf Club layout regularly since 1938, couldn't remember if Franklin Roosevelt or Harry Truman was president when he made his first ace. He knew Bill Clinton was president when he made his second one, however. White believed his first hole-in-one was in 1947, but there is no record to confirm that fact.

"It was in the 1940s, but I don't remember what year," White said. "I forget a lot of stuff."

It just so happened that the same day White made his hole-in-one, I was playing in the Colonial Wide Open, Colonial Country Club's annual media golf tournament in Fort Worth. One of my playing partners was John Lumpkin, the Dallas bureau chief for the Associated Press. A couple of weeks later, Lumpkin was in Abilene and stopped by my office to talk golf. I told him the story of White's hole-in-one and gave him a copy of the column I had written about it.

He sent the column to AP staff writer Mark Babineck in Lubbock. Babineck went to Anson and wrote a feature on White. Don Cronin from *USA Today* then called me for some additional information. He had seen the AP story on White and was writing a story of his own about the hole-in-one for that national publication.

White died a little more than two years later at age ninety-three, but his hole-in-one was not forgotten after his story was published in newspapers all over the country. He is still fondly remembered in his hometown, too. The No. 6 hole at Anson Golf Club has been renamed "Hoolie's Hole," and the club's annual "Sponsors' Classic" golf tournament held each October has been renamed the "Hoolie" in memory of White.

Finally, there is the story of Fred Lee Hughes, a second-generation car dealer and former Abilene mayor. Hughes said his company, Fred Hughes Motors, had offered a new car for a hole-in-one in tournaments for years but had never given one away.

That changed on June 24, 1994, during the Lee Medical Supply Charity Golf Tournament, benefiting Hospice of Abilene. Fred Hughes Motors offered a 1994 Buick LeSabre for a hole-in-one at the par-three, 179-yard tenth hole at Abilene Country Club.

Guess who hit the hole-in-one to win the car? That's right, Hughes himself, using a seven-wood.

"I'm going to give it to Wanda, my wife, because she needs one," Hughes quipped when asked after the tournament what he was going to do with the car.

Five days later, Paul Harvey included a story of Hughes' hole-in-one on his nationally syndicated radio show.

"Fred Hughes of Abilene, Texas, donated a Buick LeSabre for a hole-in-one," Harvey announced, "and then he won it."

Now, you know the rest of the story.

The NFL's Forgotten Fatality

Every time there is a heat-related death in a National Football League training camp, or a serious spinal injury like the one that Reggie Brown, the Detroit Lion and former Texas A&M linebacker suffered in the final regular-season game of the 1997 season, the nation's sports pages and airwaves are filled with stories about similar incidents that had occurred previously.

Fortunately, Brown's story had a happy ending as he miraculously walked to the podium to speak at a press conference just weeks after his injury. In the days following Brown's injury, however, obvious comparisons had been drawn to another former Lion, Mike Utley, as well as other NFL players such as Darryl Stingley, who were left paralyzed by spinal injuries.

No mention at the time, however, was made of the death of another former Detroit Lions player twenty-

Chuck Hughes (13) was a star receiver at Texas Western before playing in the NFL. Courtesy of the University of Texas-El Paso sports information office.

six years earlier. It is believed to be the last game-related death of an NFL player.

The date was October 24, 1971. Wide receiver Chuck Hughes, a native Texan whose story of his life and career is nearly as remarkable as his death was tragic, was returning to the huddle in the closing minutes of the Lions' 28-23 loss to the Chicago Bears when he collapsed on the Bears' fifteen-yard line and lay motionless.

Team physicians administered mouth-to-mouth resuscitation and external heart massage before Hughes was put on a stretcher and taken to nearly Henry Ford Hospital in Detroit. He died minutes later in the hospital.

Stories in the next day's paper said it was believed that Hughes died of a ruptured major vessel of the aorta, the heart or possibly the brain. Later, an autopsy revealed that Hughes had heart damage, similar to someone in his seventies or eighties, not a healthy twenty-eight-year-old NFL wide receiver. Amazingly, no physical examinations during his five seasons in the NFL had revealed his heart ailment.

Wally Bullington, who had been Hughes' high school coach in Abilene, remembers the day well when he learned of Hughes' death.

"I was always impressed with his self-discipline," recalled Bullington, who later served as the head football coach and athletic director at Abilene Christian University.

Indeed, Hughes' story was an unusual one. His father died in 1949 and his mother in 1958. So Chuck, the eleventh of sixteen children, lived with his older brother Tom while he attended Abilene High. Hughes played wide receiver for the Eagles as a junior in 1961. He was not eligible to play as a senior, however, because he had turned nineteen before the start of the season. But instead of giving up the sport, Hughes worked out with the team and served as a student coach.

"He was a hard worker," Bullington said. "He really wanted to play college football. He always had good hands, but no one thought about him playing pro football since he was so skinny. A lot of kids would have quit, but he never let up. He really wanted to go to college and play football."

Hughes began to grow and improve his speed during his senior year. Through the help of Bullington and legendary former Abilene High coach Chuck Moser, Hughes was given a tryout at Texas-El Paso, then called Texas Western, and received a scholarship.

At Texas Western he became known as the "Abilene Whippet" for his size, stamina and speed. He set eight school receiving records for the Miners and was then drafted by the Philadelphia Eagles in 1967. He played three seasons as a reserve before the Lions acquired him for a draft choice before the 1970 season.

Chuck Hughes still holds several UTEP receiving records. Courtesy of the University of Texas-El Paso sports information office.

In the fall of 2006, Texas-El Paso remembered Hughes by naming him to the school's athletics hall of fame. UTEP's biography of Hughes at the hall of fame banquet cited the many remarkable accomplishments of his collegiate career:

"One of the most prolific receivers in school history, Chuck Hughes played for the Miners from 1964-1966. He helped the team to fourteen victories, including a Sun Bowl victory in 1965. The Abilene, Texas, native reeled in a school-record eighty catches for 1,519 yards in 1965, the best total in program annals, to garner All-America status. Hughes' seventeen receptions against Arizona State and his 349 yards against North Texas, an NCAA record at the time, highlighted the sensational season. His 34.9 yards per reception versus North Texas still stands as an NCAA record. The 1965 campaign was capped off in stellar fashion, as Hughes snared six passes for 115 yards against TCU in the Sun Bowl.

"Hughes had 162 catches during his prolific career, including nineteen touchdown grabs. He also was a terror in the return game, compiling 272 yards and one score on twelve career punt returns and bringing back thirty-six kickoffs for another 851 yards. Hughes led the team in receiving on twenty-one occasions, eclipsing the 100-yard barrier a school-record thirteen times."

From having to sit out his senior year in high school to a record-breaking collegiate career and then five seasons in the NFL, Hughes' remarkable rags-to-riches story has unfortunately been forgotten over the last three-plus decades. Sadly, even his untimely death, the last game-related death in an NFL game, has been seemingly overlooked by the national media.

It is, however, a story that needs to be remembered.

Great Texas
Basketball Games

Texas is known as a football state, but there have been plenty of important basketball games played in the Lone Star State.

The San Antonio Spurs have won four of the last nine National Basketball Association championships. The Houston Rockets won two NBA titles during that same time frame, and the Dallas Mavericks played in the 2006 NBA Finals. Both Dallas and San Antonio have played host to NCAA Final Fours.

But I will make the argument that two of the most significant games in the history of basketball were played in Texas, and neither had anything to do with the aforementioned NBA Finals or NCAA Final Four.

One is pretty obvious—the contest between UCLA and the University of Houston that was played on January 20, 1968. The other may be a little less identifiable because it was overshadowed by an even more historical game a week later.

First, the game in Houston in 1968. UCLA, the defending national champion led by Lew Alcindor (who later became known at Kareem Abdul-Jabbar), was riding a forty-seven-game winning streak. Houston, paced by all-American Elvin Hayes, had run off a string of sixteen straight wins to open the season. The Cougars also entered the game protecting a forty-eight-game home winning streak.

Only this game was not played on the Cougars' on-campus home court at Hofheinz Arena. Instead, the game was moved to the Astrodome and played in front of 52,693 fans.

Today, much of what happened in that marquee match up seems routine, but the 1968 game between the Cougars and Bruins marked a number of "firsts" for the sport. It was the first regular-season game ever to be seen on national television, televised live in primetime on a Saturday night. It was also the first game to be played in a domed stadium, a regular occurrence for Final Four and other NCAA tournament games today.

Houston pulled off the stunner as Hayes hit a pair of free throws with twenty-eight seconds left to give the Cougars a 71-69 upset of UCLA. Although the Bruins gained revenge by beating Houston a couple of months later in the Final Four semifinals, the game set a precedence for much that has followed over the last forty years as college basketball and March Madness has grown in popularity.

The other historically significant game in Texas took place in Lubbock. The 1966 NCAA Midwest Regional was held at the old Lubbock Municipal Coliseum. When the twenty-two-team NCAA Tournament began in 1966, Kentucky was ranked number one, Duke number two and Kansas number four. Surprising upstart Texas Western, now known as the University of Texas-El Paso, was rated number three, but no one expected the Miners to be able to contend with such traditional powers as Kentucky, Duke and Kansas.

Texas Western had to go overtime in the Midwest Regional semifinals, edging Cincinnati 78-76. That set up the classic regional championship game between Kansas and Texas Western, a game that featured controversy and set the stage for perhaps the most socially significant sporting event of the last century.

The Miners upset Kansas and all-American guard Jo Jo White in an 81-80 double-overtime thriller. At the end of the first overtime, White hit a long shot from the sideline that seemingly won the game for Kansas, but the official ruled that White's foot was barely on the out-of-bounds line.

Much has been written about that call over the years. In fact, the *Kansas City Star* ran a lengthy feature a few years ago, talking to the players, coaches and even Rick Clarkson, the noted sports photographer who shot a picture of White's shot. The photo was inconclusive as to whether White's foot was actually on the line or if he was on his toes, with his heel in the air above the line but not touching it.

Retrospectives have tended to fall along the lines of whether you were rooting for the Miners or the Jayhawks.

On the *Lawrence Journal-World's* KUsports.com website, Ken Johnson writes, "White actually won the game on a last-season shot, but a ref ruled that he stepped out of bounds (film later showed he was at least six inches in). Ah, what could have been."

Moe Iba, assistant coach to Don Haskins on Texas Western, was asked about the call in 2006 during on on-line review of the movie *Glory Road*.

"The thing was we were very fortunate to win because they had Jo Jo White and Walt Wesley, meaning they had size and a great point guard," Iba said. "And, both teams I thought played very well the whole ballgame. We were very fortunate that the referee was in the right spot at the right time when Jo Jo stepped on the line and hit the shot that would have beaten us."

Texas Western, of course, did win the game and then advanced to the Final Four at Cole Fieldhouse on the University of Maryland campus where the Miners upset top-ranked Kentucky 72-65 in a game that would forever change college basketball.

Haskins played five African-American players against an all-white Kentucky team. Haskins and the Miners shocked the basketball world, effectively ending segregation in college basketball in the South and disproving the racist notion that five black players couldn't beat five white players. That game is credited with not only changing college basketball but also changing America.

As for the call that night in Lubbock that wiped out White's game-winning shot, Haskins wrote in his book *Glory Road*, which was the basis for the movie by the same name, "Then at the end of the first OT, with the score tied at 71, White threw in a jump shot right at the buzzer. On television it looked good, but he had a foot on the out-of-bounds line and the basket got waved off. It was the right call, but this is how close we came to losing."

How different history books would read if Texas Western hadn't beaten Kentucky in the 1966 national championship game. But if it hadn't been a controversial call a week earlier in Lubbock, the Miners wouldn't have even been in the game that changed basketball forever.

The Greatest Game
Never Played

···

Imagine how different life was for the sports fan in Texas in 1913.

It would be another year before the Southwest Conference, long the staple of sports in Texas, was first organized. It would be seven more years before the Texas Interscholastic League, now known as the University Interscholastic League, held its first state high school football championship game.

The National Football League hadn't yet been formed. Neither had the National Basketball Association. Not only had television not yet been invented, but neither had radio. Life in 1913 was pre-World War I, pre-television, pre-radio, pre-talking movies, pre-women's suffrage.

Indeed, baseball was the national pastime because it was really the only sport. Major league baseball had only sixteen teams in 1913, and none was located farther west than St. Louis, home to both the Cardinals and Browns.

For baseball fans in Texas, their heroes were baseball stars whom most had never seen and only read about in the newspaper. So imagine the excitement when it was announced that the New York Giants and Chicago White Sox, following the 1913 season, were going to stage a barnstorming tour that would come through Texas.

Barnstorming was a common practice in those days, allowing players to earn extra money by playing exhibition games in places that normally didn't have the opportunity to see major league baseball.

But there had never been a barnstorming tour as ambitious as the one put together by White Sox owner Charles Comiskey and Giants manager John McGraw in a tavern in Chicago in December 1912. The two teams were scheduled to go on a forty-nine-game world tour, playing thirty-one games in thirty-three days in the United States before boarding a steamer in Vancouver to sail overseas for games in Japan, China, Phillippines, Australia, Belgium, France, Germany, Ireland, England, and Scotland. The White Sox and Giants played before King George V of England and Pope Pius X at the Vatican before returning to New York harbor on March 6, 1914, ending a five-month tour.

After the Philadelphia Phillies beat the Giants in the fifth and deciding game of the World Series on October 13, 1913, Comiskey and McGraw filled out their rosters with players from other teams and then started the tour in Cincinnati on October 18.

Games in Texas were scheduled in Bonham, Dallas, Beaumont, Houston, Marlin, Abilene, and El Paso. Major league baseball wasn't totally foreign to Texans in 1913. Although the majors didn't put a team in Texas until the formation of the Houston Colt '45s in 1962, the Lone Star State was home to spring training in those days. In fact, seventeen different Texas cities hosted spring training sites for major league teams between 1903 and 1941.

McGraw's Giants trained in Marlin, a small community near Waco that was then known as Marlin Springs for its mineral water, from 1908-1918. The Philadelphia A's also trained in San Antonio and the St. Louis Browns in Waco in 1913.

Abilene had never hosted a big-league spring training camp, however, so the upcoming game between the Giants and White Sox was just about the biggest thing to ever happen in that West Texas railroad town that had been organized just thirty-two years earlier.

The local newspaper billed it "the greatest game of baseball ever played in Central West Texas." The Abilene Young Men's Booster Club, headed up by secretary Fred T. Wood, put up $1,000 and guaranteed the two teams eighty percent of the gate to land a game in Abilene on November 4, 1913.

The day had been declared a holiday in Abilene. Schools dismissed at one o'clock and the city's businesses closed from one to four. Full-page ads in the *Abilene Daily Reporter* in the weeks leading up to the game advertised "special excursion" rates on the railroad for those outside of Abilene to come to the game. Special trains were scheduled to bring fans from as far away as Cisco and Sweetwater (fifty and forty-two miles, respectively).

Tickets were one dollar for adults and seventy-five cents for students. A new grandstand was built at Simmons College Park, and forty-one boxes were constructed, protected by a twelve-foot wire netting. The newspaper said the game was expected to attract 5,000 people. College students from Simmons cleaned the park, getting the field in "tip-top shape." Parking was prepared for twenty-five cars.

There was only one problem. The game never took place. When the Texas & Pacific Special, carrying the two teams from their game in Marlin the day before, arrived at 4:40 that morning at the T&P Depot across the Hotel Grace in downtown Abilene, it was already raining. By game time at two, six-tenths of an inch of rain had fallen in Abilene and the Simmons Park field was declared unplayable.

Some of the players never even got off the train. Others mingled with the fans in businesses in downtown Abilene. Christy Mathewson, the best pitcher in baseball at the time, had been scheduled to pitch that day in Abilene. Outfielder Jim Thorpe, who had signed with the Giants earlier in the year after he was forced to return his two 1912 Olympic gold medals, was also scheduled to play that day for the Giants.

Thorpe won the decathlon and pentathlon in Stockholm in 1912, but in January of 1913 the International Olympic Committee and the U.S. Olympic Committee learned that Thorpe had played minor league baseball in 1909 and 1910 in the Eastern Carolina League. He had reportedly been paid thirty dollars a month, a violation of the Olympic Games' strict amateur code.

The White Sox lineup had five future Hall of Famers in its line-up, including native Texan outfielder Tris Speaker of the Boston Red Sox, Sam Crawford, Red Faber, noted strikeout pitcher Walter Johnson, and Ray Schalk.

The *Daily Reporter*, Abilene's afternoon paper, wrote, "And it rained! There was many a disappointed fan in the city of Abilene and many others who do not reside here, when weather conditions became such that the scheduled game between the Giants and White Sox could not be played. Since the announcement that the game had been secured for Abilene, this day had been looked forward to by all lovers of the National sport, and there was keen disappointment on every hand when it became fact that the game could not be staged."

The teams then re-boarded the train and headed for El Paso and its next game, possibly enjoying their first day off after contests on seventeen consecutive days. But for baseball fans in Abilene, it was the "Greatest Game Never Played."

Sweetwater's Best

Sweetwater bills itself as home to the "World's Largest Rattlesnake Roundup." But Sweetwater, a small city located forty-two miles west of Abilene on Interstate 20, can also call itself home to two of the greatest football players in National Football League history.

Sammy Baugh and Clyde "Bulldog" Turner, both Sweetwater High School graduates, are both members of the Pro Football Hall of Fame. They are also the answer to a trivia question: Name the first two head coaches of the New York Jets.

When the fledgling American Football League began in 1960, New York Titans owner, Harry Wismer talked Baugh into taking the job as the team's new coach. Years later, Baugh called the decision to take the job with the Titans the biggest mistake of his life.

Baugh, you see, had been coaching at tiny Hardin-Simmons University in Abilene since his retirement from the Washington Redskins in 1952. Abilene was just an hour's drive from his beloved 7,667-acre Double Mountain Ranch, located between Rotan and Aspermont, that he bought in 1941. Coaching at Hardin-Simmons allowed Baugh to coach football yet continue to live on his ranch.

He didn't dislike coaching pro football. He just hated living in New York City. He preferred the wide-open spaces of West Texas, where he could chew tobacco, wear blue jeans and boots, and talk about the weather and raise his cattle, just like his neighbors.

Baugh coached the Titans to back-to-back 7-7 seasons. When he decided that he had enough of life in New York City, he left to become an assistant with the Houston Oilers. But Baugh talked Wismer into hiring fellow Sweetwater native Turner as his replacement.

Turner stayed just one season. Sonny Werblin bought out the financially strapped Wismer the next year, changed the team's nickname to the Jets, hired Weeb Ewbank to replace Turner, and drafted a quarterback from Alabama who became known as "Broadway Joe." The Jets paid out an unheard-of-sum of $427,000 for Joe Namath, who in 1968 led the Jets to a Super Bowl title.

While Baugh, the only remaining living member of the inaugural class of the Pro Football Hall of Fame, has been the subject of numerous books and stories, Turner has seemingly been forgotten.

But as a center and linebacker in the era of two-way players in the NFL, he was one of the game's greatest. Like Baugh, he was inducted into both the College and Pro Football Halls of Fame.

Born five years after Baugh, Turner went from Sweetwater to Hardin-Simmons in nearby Abilene to play college football. The Chicago Bears made him their first pick in the 1940 NFL draft.

Life was different in those days. George Richards, the owner of the Detroit Lions, wanted his team to draft Turner with its first pick. Gus Henderson, Detroit's head coach, didn't, however, so the Bears selected Turner with the seventh pick of the first round.

But Richards, who had first met Turner when Hardin-Simmons played a game against Loyola of Los Angeles in the fall of 1939, didn't give up on trying to acquire Turner for his team. Years later, in an interview with Pittsburgh-based writer Myron Cope, Turner described Richards' attempt to pry him away from the Bears:

"He said, 'You're still going to be with the Lions,'" Turner recalled. "'You just tell the Bears you're not going to play pro football. I'll make you a coach at a high school out here in California for the first year, and after George Halas gives up on you, you come with the Lions.'"

Turner said he flew to Chicago to meet with Halas after the draft, but he didn't sign immediately with the Bears. Richards found out about Turner's trip to Chicago and was mad.

"He came down to Abilene, Mr. Richards himself did, and registered incognito," Turner continued in his interview with Cope. "Now I had a friend on the newspaper, Hershell Schooley, and I told Hershell, 'George Richards that owns the Detroit Lions is in town and he wants to talk to me tonight.' Well, you can't tell a newspaperman secrets. Hershell said, 'I'm going with you,' and carried a pad and pencil. We went up there to the room, and Mr. Richards came out of the shower with a towel wrapped around him and he said, 'Who is this?' I said, 'A reporter!' And man, he hit the ceiling. He said, 'I've come all the way from California incognito, and you bring a newspaperman here?' Hershell said. 'Why, you old S.O.B.,' and I had to step in and cool the smoke down. Anyway, we finally worked it out that Mr. Richards was going to send me $100 a month until something happened on the high school coaching job. But real soon after that I asked them to quit sending me the $100. Mr. Richards promised me the world, and I'm sure he would have kept his promise, but I signed with the Bears. I didn't want to lay out a year.

"Then the league found out that George Richards had been trying to get me, and they fined him $5,000 for tampering with me after I was drafted by the Bears. They said Mr. Richards had spent $500 getting my teeth fixed. Well, that wasn't the truth. He never spent anything on my teeth. He sold his ball club and got out of football, and it was an injustice, because he had never spent a nickel on my teeth."

Turner played for the Bears from 1940-1952. At 6'2", 235 pounds, he was big for his era. A six-time all-pro center and a steady linebacker, Turner intercepted four passes in five NFL title games for the league's powerhouse Bears. In 1942, he led the league with eight interceptions, including picking off Baugh, his fellow Sweetwater Mustang. Baugh introduced Turner when the latter was inducted into Hardin-Simmons' Athletic Hall of Honor.

Turner was named to the NFL's 1940s All-Decade Team. He died in 1998 in his home in Gatesville at the age of seventy-nine.

Rancher and Football Star

He is known to millions of football fans as "Slinging Sammy," a legendary figure they have only heard of but never saw play. To Bob O'Day and other West Texans, however, he was simply known as Sam.

Sweetwater's Sam Baugh is still considered one of the greatest quarterbacks in NFL history. From the author's collection.

Make a list of the greatest football legends to ever come out of Texas, Sam Baugh would be at the top of a short list. Baugh, inducted as a member of the inaugural class of the Pro Football Hall of Fame in 1963 in Canton, Ohio, is considered the father of the modern forward pass in the National Football League.

He quarterbacked Texas Christian University in the first Cotton Bowl, and his bust sits atop the Cotton Bowl trophy. He spent sixteen seasons with the Washington Redskins in the National Football League. In 1943, Baugh led the NFL in passing, punting and interceptions. He still holds the two NFL records for season punting average (51.4 yards) and career punting average (45.1 yards), more than a half century after he retired. He was the first coach of the New York Titans, now known as the Jets, and he later coached the Houston Oilers for one season. He even filmed some Western serials in Hollywood, which got a real cowboy when Baugh played the part on the big screen.

For more than sixty years—until poor health forced him to move to a nursing home as he approached his ninetieth birthday—home for Baugh was the Double Mountain Ranch, a 7,667-spread between Rotan and Aspermont in a rugged, sparsely populated stretch of West Texas that some have referred to as the "Big Empty."

Baugh was just a West Texas rancher who happened to be one of the greatest football players of all time.

From 1977 until Baugh's health declined in 2004, Bob O'Day and Baugh played golf together three or four times a week at the Western Texas College course in Snyder. The golf course has since been renamed the Sammy Baugh Golf Course, just as Snyder Avenue, the main street in Rotan, is now called Sammy Baugh Avenue. A children's home in nearby Jayton also carries his name.

"Sam came over to Snyder to play golf three to four times a week," said O'Day, who spent thirty years coaching in Snyder, including eleven years as the golf coach at Western Texas College. "From his ranch to the Western Texas College course is fifty miles one way. He drove 300 to 400 miles a week for twenty-seven years."

O'Day said Baugh would often come over early and just sit around the pro shop talking to people.

"I think that is why Sam liked coming to Snyder," O'Day said, "because people treated him like one of the boys, an old West Texas rancher. Sam liked people, but he didn't much like cities. He was a good storyteller, but he never talked much about himself. He'd always talk about other great players, like Dick Todd or Bulldog Turner."

O'Day said football fans would often come to Snyder, just to play golf with Baugh. Fifteen years ago, I was fortunate to play eighteen holes with Baugh and O'Day. It remains a highlight of my career. Baugh talked about how the game of football had changed since he first started in the NFL in 1937.

"The rules are so different now," he said. "If you got hurt on the opening kickoff, you couldn't come back in until the second quarter. They had some of the craziest rules I ever heard of when I first came into the league."

Each NFL team carried only twenty-three-man rosters then. All players played both ways, on offense and defense. During his sixteen seasons with the Redskins, Baugh saw a change in the style of offenses, from the single wing to the T-formation. He also saw many rule changes, including the allowance of free substitution and the advent of two-platoon football. But Baugh claimed the biggest change during his career related to passing.

"When I first started, the passer had to be five yards behind the line of scrimmage," he said. "There was no protection for the passers. They could hit the passer until the whistle blew to stop play. Defensive backs could hit a receiver until the ball was in the air. The NFL was a defensive game and a running game."

Many credit Baugh's performance as a rookie in the 1937 NFL title game for changing the league's rules concerning passing quarterbacks. He threw three touchdown passes in the championship game as the Redskins beat Chicago 28-21.

"I don't know if that game changed things," Baugh said, "but after that they started drafting quarterbacks who could throw. Mr. (George) Marshall (Washington Redskins owner) and George Halas (Chicago Bears coach and owner) got the rules changed to help the passer."

For example, the fifteen-yard roughing-the-passer rule was adopted in 1938. Of course, Marshall and Halas had a vested interest in such changes—Marshall had Baugh and two years later the Bears acquired Sid Luckman.

Before that rule change, "They'd chase me eighty yards all over the field," Baugh said, "trying to hit me after I'd thrown the ball. I learned to pass on the move. They finally realized that people wanted to see scoring and the passing game. In sixteen years in the NFL, I never had a coach tell me to throw the ball away. That's why there were more interceptions then. Quarterbacks didn't throw the ball away. Back then, offensive lineman couldn't use their hands at all. Every rule now helps the passing game."

Despite those old rules, Baugh still holds the Washington record for career touchdowns with 187, and his career passing yardage (22,085) ranks third behind Joe Theismann (25,206) and Sonny Jurgenson (22,585). As a defensive back, he intercepted thirty-one passes, ranking third on the Redskins' career list behind Darrell Green and Brig Owens. Baugh once threw for 446 yards in a game—still a Washington record.

Despite those many accomplishments, Baugh considered himself first and foremost a common, everyday West Texas rancher.

O'Day has two favorite stories concerning his golf partner. Baugh was inducted into the Cotton Bowl Hall of Fame in 1999 along with former Arkansas coach Frank Broyles, former Texas quarterback James Street, former Houston football player David Hodge, former sports writer Felix McKnight and Gussie Davis, the longtime sponsor of the Kilgore Rangerettes.

O'Day and Baugh's son Todd represented him at the induction ceremony that day, and O'Day said he was given two footballs, one for himself and one for Sam, that had the signatures of each of the inductees lasered on it. O'Day gave Sam his football the next day at the pro shop at the Western Texas College golf course. Baugh saw a young boy in the pro shop and handed him the football

"Here, you'll have more use for this than me," Baugh told the eight-year-old.

Sports Illustrated, in its annual football preview edition, several years ago asked some of the stars of the NFL what former star they would like to meet and then got the two together. Indianapolis Colts quarterback Peyton Manning selected Baugh, and Manning and a photographer came out to the Double Mountain Ranch to meet him. Manning and Baugh were pictured together in that *Sports Illustrated* issue.

"I was there that day," O'Day said. "Peyton and Sam sat and talked for more than two hours. After that Peyton would call Sam occasionally to talk to him. Sam thought a lot of him, what a nice young man he was."

A couple of months after the Colts' victory in Super Bowl XLI in 2007, O'Day said his phone rang and it was Archie Manning, Peyton's father, inquiring about Sam. He sent O'Day a Colts' Super Bowl cap that O'Day took to Baugh in the nursing home.

"He smiled when I gave it to him, and I imagine he's wearing it now," O'Day said. "He always wears a cap. Archie said Peyton has a wall in the basement of his house with pictures of quarterbacks he admires. In the middle is a picture of Sam."

Sam Baugh: football star, Texas legend and rancher—although if you ask his friends and golfing partners—not necessarily in that order.

Longhorns Helping Sooners?

Can you imagine the University of Texas coaching staff purposely giving its playbook to the rival Oklahoma Sooners? Seems about as likely as the United States and Soviet Union cooperatively trading secrets during the Cold War, but it did happen.

To set the stage for that unusual occurrence, let's go back a couple of years earlier. Emory Bellard, one of only a few high school coaches to later become a head football coach in the Southwest Conference, had an impressive 218-81-14 record in twenty-seven seasons as a high school coach. He won back-to-back state titles at Breckenridge in 1958 and 1959 and then captured another state championship at San Angelo Central in 1966 before legendary Texas coach Darrell Royal hired Bellard to join his staff in Austin.

Emory Bellard is credited with inventing the wishbone offense. Courtesy of Big Country Hall of Fame, Texas State Technical College, West Texas.

"My first year (1967) I coached the linebackers for (defensive coordinator) Mike Campbell," recalled Bellard. "At the end of the spring that next year (1968), Darrell reorganized the staff and put me in charge of the offense."

Bellard, famous for constantly drawing X's and O's on graph paper, had been tinkering with an idea for a new offense. So that summer, after spring practice had concluded, Bellard took his son and a number of players who had completed their eligibility but were still in Austin attending summer school, down on the field at Memorial Stadium to demonstrate his new offense to Royal.

"I used them (the former players) to see if I could get the reads (on the triple option) like I thought I could," said Bellard, who even broke a finger on a bad snap during the demonstration. "Darrell liked it, and he OK'd it."

The Longhorns installed the new offense that fall. So how effective was it?

"We tied the first game, lost the second and won the next thirty," responded Bellard, who admitted he had been working on his nameless three-back, triple-option offense for years. "The lead halfback could block at three different points in the defensive structure. The relationship of the two halfbacks, the lead halfback and the pitch halfback, were in perfect relationship, and the quarterback wasn't making blind pitches. It had perfect balance. You could run the same play both directions."

Although Bellard didn't have a name for his new offense, veteran Houston sports writer Mickey Herskowitz coined the phrase "the wishbone" for Bellard's alignment, since the fullback was directly behind the quarterback and slightly in front of the two halfbacks, making it look like a wishbone.

"The offense is a truly sound offense," said Bellard, still excited to talk about his creation as he approaches his eightieth birthday. "It is not a gimmick. It is built on sound principles. It is the winningest formation in the history of football."

Bellard, who compiled an 89-71 record in fourteen seasons as the head coach at Texas A&M and Mississippi State after his time on Royal's staff at Texas, noted that Alabama, Oklahoma and Texas all won multiple national championships using the wishbone.

Texas used its wishbone for a late drive, capped by Steve Worster's seven-yard touchdown run, to beat Oklahoma 26-20 in 1968. The Longhorns whipped the Sooners again in 1969 (27-17) and 1970 (41-9). In the spring of 1969, however, Royal came into Bellard's office.

"Chuck Fairbanks (Oklahoma's head coach) is in bad trouble," Royal told Bellard. "I think he is fixing to get fired. I want to help Chuck. Barry Switzer (OU's offensive coordinator) is going to call you. I want you to tell him how to run the wishbone."

"You just want me to show them how we line up?" Bellard asked.

"No, I want you to give them everything you know about running the wishbone," Royal responded.

So Bellard "gave" Oklahoma his wishbone offense, and the Sooners quickly became the nation's most prolific running attack. Over the next six years, Oklahoma's wishbone beat Texas' wishbone five straight years and the two teams tied in 1976, Royal's final season before retiring.

"Darrell called me about a year ago," said Bellard, and the two former coaches reminisced about the day they gave their wishbone playbook to rival Oklahoma. "He said, 'I wouldn't be nearly as benevolent now as I was then.'"

No, You Take It

I f John Abendschan, the head football coach at Boswell High School in suburban Fort Worth, wants to tell his team about unusual plays in football, all he needs to do is call on his father. I'm not sure if anyone has ever been involved in a more unusual play than Jack Abendschan.

Ever seen a football player field a kick and then punt it back to the other team, only to have it kicked back to him? No, me neither, but it really happened in a professional football game.

Now retired from the insurance business and a high school and college football coaching career in Texas, Jack Abendschan played for the Saskatchewan Rough Riders in the Canadian Football League after an all-American career as an offensive lineman and place-kicker at the University of New Mexico.

Cleveland Browns offensive lineman Lou Groza and Oakland Raiders quarterback George Blanda were probably the last two players in the National Football League to play a position and also serve as their team's place-kicker. But Abendschan, who had a tryout with the Denver Broncos in 1967, is believed to be the last pro football player to handle both duties, playing both offensive line and kicking during his ten seasons (1965-1975) with Saskatchwean.

He was the CFL Western Conference scoring champion in 1968, a five-time all-CFL selection and played in four Grey Cups—Canada's Super Bowl—helping the Rough Riders win the championship in 1966. He was named to the Saskatchewan Wall of Honor in 1992.

The most unusual play in Abendschan's career involved the rouge, a unique CFL rule that gives a team a point if a punt, kick-off or missed field goal goes out of the back of the end zone or fails to be returned out of the end zone. That is a little more difficult than it sounds because the end zone in the Canadian Football League is twenty-five yards deep.

"The game was tied and we got in position for a field goal at the end of the game," recalled Abendschan, whose longest field goal of his career was fifty-two yards. "It was a short one, only about thirty-five yards. I thought all I had to do was kick it out of the end zone for rouge and we'd win by one point. But I hit it low. Their guy caught the ball and punted it so he wouldn't be tackled in the end zone. Our quarterback caught it and punted it back to the same guy in the end zone.

"He punted it again and our fullback caught it. There is a rule in the Canadian League which says a defender can't be within five yards of a player catching a punt. In all the melee, a Winnipeg player was within five yards of our fullback. The game can't end on a penalty, so we lined up again and I kicked a field goal to win the game and put us in the Grey Cup."

Indeed, sometimes fact is stranger than fiction.

The Amazing Matadors

New high schools have opened almost every fall across the state over the last fifty-plus years as Texas continues to experience remarkable growth. But no new school—before

Hardin-Simmons Coach Jimmie Keeling led Lubbock Estacado to a state championship in 1968. Courtesy of Hardin-Simmons University sports information office.

or since—has accomplished what Lubbock Estacado High School did in 1968, winning a state championship in its first season of varsity football.

Jimmie Keeling, the architect of that remarkable Estacado team, has since built another "miracle," taking a new program at Hardin-Simmons University and turning it into the winningest college football team in Texas.

The Associated Press and *Texas Monthly* magazine both ran stories in 2006 about Keeling and Hardin-Simmons, which hadn't fielded a football team in twenty-seven years until hiring Keeling in 1990. Since re-starting a football program at the small Baptist college in Abilene, Keeling compiled a 143-41 record in seventeen seasons. That is more wins than Texas, Texas A&M, Texas A&M-Kingsville or any other college football program in the state during the same time period. And Keeling is still going strong, despite passing the normal retirement ages of sixty-five and seventy.

He has won ten conference titles and ranks among the top ten Division III coaches in the nation in winning percentage. Keeling also compiled a 196-91-11 mark in thirty years as a high school coach before taking the Hardin-Simmons job and was named to the Texas High School Coaches Association Hall of Honor in 1995.

The Associated Press and *Texas Monthly* articles failed to mention what he and his Estacado team accomplished in 1968. The "Estacado Miracle" may top all his other achievements.

Estacado High School actually opened its doors in the fall of 1967, but the Matadors, made up of mostly freshmen and sophomores, played a junior varsity schedule. The next year, the team, still fielding a lineup of primarily sophomores and juniors, played its first varsity football game.

"We won the first game 14-0," Kenneth Wallace, the team's quarterback, told the *Lubbock Avalanche-Journal* in a retrospective feature in 2003. "We won the last game 14-0 and we finished the season 14-0. I guess it was just meant to be."

Did Keeling have any idea what was about to happen when the Matadors took the field for the season opener against heavily favored Brownfield?

"We realized we had a lot of committed guys who worked in a special way," Keeling said. "We weren't that big, but we had a lot of quickness."

My, how those Matadors could play defense! Estacado outscored its first five opponents 195-0 and completed its run through district (all ten games were district games that season) by giving up only twelve points while scoring 431 points.

"We had two huge games (during the regular season)," Keeling recalled "Brownfield was an outstanding team, and we won 14-0 in the opener. That was a positive start. Then we played Sweetwater in the final game. Both teams were undefeated. Sweetwater had lost the opener to Lubbock Dunbar the year before and had then won eighteen in a row."

Estacado edged Sweetwater 7-0 in rough-and-tumble defensive struggle.

"In my mind, that was for the state championship," David Moody, a former team member who later coached at Estacado, told the Lubbock newspaper. "We knew whoever won that game would have a chance to win it all. That was one of the most physical games I've ever played in."

In between those two bookend wins against Brownfield and Sweetwater, Estacado piled up victories of 51-0 over Littlefield, 33-0 over Lamesa, 69-0 over Levelland, 28-0 over Dunbar, 73-6 over San Angelo Lake View, 60-6 over Slaton, 54-0 over Snyder and 42-0 over Colorado City.

And now it was time for the playoffs. First up on the schedule was a Thanksgiving Day match up at Shotwell Stadium in Abilene against Brownwood, ranked number one in the state and guided by legendary coach Gordon Wood. The Matadors rolled to a 49-8 victory over the Lions.

Estacado followed that with a 28-12 win over Kermit, setting up a showdown with Henderson, led by running back Joe Wylie, who became an all-American at Oklahoma.

"I remember the week in practice before that game, one of our guys, Willie Avery, was designated to be Joe Wylie," Wallace recalled in the *Lubbock Avalanche-Journal* story. "I mean we tagged Willie all week. I don't see how he was able to play in that game."

But Avery and the Estacado defense did play. The Matadors held Wylie to sixteen yards rushing in a 30-0 victory.

That set up the state championship game against Refugio at TCU's Amon Carter Stadium in Fort Worth. A goal-line stand late in the first half proved critical.

"They had the ball inside the six-inch line and didn't score," Keeling said. "In fact, I think they ended up on the seven- or eight-yard line."

Estacado scored fourteen first-half points. Its defense had the goal-line stand and then shut out Refugio in the second half to claim a 14-0 victory, a Class 3A state championship and an undefeated season. Estacado, the only school ever to win a state football championship in its first varsity season, outscored its opponents 552-32.

"It was a lot of fun," said Keeling, looking back on that remarkable 1968 season. "It was exciting. The hardest thing (about starting a new program) is the technical aspect of getting equipment and doing all the things that everybody else already has a place."

Keeling used that experience when he started the program at Hardin-Simmons.

"It had a lot to do with me having confidence to begin a program," he said. "It was a big factor to learn from that experience."

Jimmie Keeling has won ten conference titles since starting the football program at Hardin-Simmons in 1990. Courtesy of Hardin-Simmons University sports information office.

Moody was asked what made the team so dominating, enjoying instantaneous success.

"If I had to put it in just a few words, we were one big family," he replied. "We went everywhere together, did everything together. And there's no doubt about it, that started with Jimmie Keeling. We had a lot of greater players, and not all of them made the team. Even though there were 1,200 or 1,300 kids in school, only thirty-eight made the varsity team. We were very fortunate to have good players, a great coaching staff and a head coach that instilled great qualities in us."

There has never been a high school football season in Texas quite like the 1968 inaugural campaign at Lubbock Estacado.

Mindy Myers from Munday

When one considers how many great athletes have come out of the state of Texas, it is a little hard to imagine that the most decorated high school athlete in the history of the

Mindy Myers Flowers is the most decorated athlete in UIL history. Courtesy of Big Country Hall of Fame, Texas State Technical College, West Texas.

University Interscholastic League is a girl who stood just 5-foot-4, weighed only 110 pounds and came from a town so small that most people living outside of West Texas have probably never heard of it.

From 1987-1990, however, Mindy Myers from Munday, Texas, was the queen of the UIL state track meet in Austin. Now Mindy Flowers, married and living near Midland, she spends much of her time these days chasing after her four children, whose ages range from five to nine. In high school, it was the rest of the state's Class A athletes who were trying to catch her.

"I entered sixteen events and won fifteen medals," Mindy said of her career at the state track meet.

Try these numbers on for size: In four trips to the state meet, Mindy won ten gold medals, three silver and two bronze. She won the 800 meters all four years in high school, captured the 1,600 meters twice, won the high jump once and anchored the Mogulettes' 1,600-meter relay team to victory three times. She also claimed silver medals in the 1,600, high jump and 400 relay and bronze medals in the high jump and 1,600.

Thanks to Mindy's efforts, Munday took second in the team standings her freshman year and then won three consecutive state team championships.

And that's not all. She also won two individual championships and had a second-place finish in leading Munday to two team titles and one second-place finish at the state meet in cross country. It would have been more, but Munday, a tiny community located halfway between Abilene and Wichita Falls, didn't field a cross country team during her freshman year.

Add to that the fact that she was named all-state in basketball and a member of the all-state tournament team as a senior when Munday reached the state semifinals, and you have the most remarkable high school athletic career in Texas history. A UIL representative hung a medal around Mindy's neck twenty-six times at a state competition.

"When you come from a school that has twenty-one in your class and then run in front of 25,000 at Memorial Stadium, that's a big thing for someone from a small town," said Mindy, when asked to list the highlight of her remarkable career.

To watch Mindy on the track was to learn the meaning of the word "competitive." She simply wouldn't let an opponent go around her, no matter how tired she was. What even the most ardent fans at the state meet, many of whom became enamored with the gutsy little girl from Munday, may not have realized, however, was that she was the youngest of fourteen children, a fact that may have impacted her success.

"I really think it made me more competitive," she said. "My dad had put up a basketball goal and poured a slab of concrete.

On Sundays when church let out, we played basketball. The big kids let me play on two conditions. I had to play by their rules, and I couldn't cry. They wouldn't let me play if I cried. I think that made me more competitive. I didn't actually grow up in Munday; I grew up in the country, and we didn't know anything except playing outside. That's all we knew. I think that influenced me. We (Mindy and her brothers and sisters) are still the worst losers."

Mindy's summer track workout consisted of running to the field to help pick watermelons.

Perhaps the best story of her competitiveness came in her junior year at the state track meet. She had been sick all weekend, and, after competing in the high jump, 800 and 1,600, she was dehydrated.

"Our coaches were pouring water on me," Mindy recalled. "Coach (Jim) Edwards said, 'It is up to you if you think you can run.' Then my sister came down. She told me, 'You're the reason this team got here, and people are counting on you. If you can run at all, you damn sure better get out there.'"

Mindy said the team was already on the track with the alternate in place to run as her substitute when she returned to the track. Her teammates began crying when they saw their anchor leg was poised to run.

"I got the baton in the lead," she said, "but another girl passed me. When you look back at the video (being filmed from the stands), you can hear our superintendent say, 'Any other time, I think Mindy would get her, but I don't think she can today.' Just then I took off and passed the other girl and you can hear him say, 'There she goes!'"

Despite being sick and competing in her fourth event of the day, Mindy anchored the 1,600-meter relay to victory and another team state championship for the Mogulettes.

"It is funny to look back on it, the whole atmosphere," she said. "It was a neat thing to be in there at Memorial Stadium."

Mindy, who played four years of college basketball at Midwestern State in Wichita Falls, has returned to the state track meet every year since 1994 to work as a volunteer official for the UIL.

"For me, it is bittersweet," she said. "The new track (at Mike Meyers Stadium, a track-only facility on the University of Texas campus) is nice, but these kids will never know what it was like to walk into Memorial Stadium with 25,000 people. Of course, it is always nice when you're winning."

Ten times in her high school career, Mindy heard those 25,000 cheering her on to victory.

When the Big Country Athletic Hall of Fame in Abilene inducted its inaugural class in 2002, a remarkable class of Pro Football Hall of Famers: quarterback Sammy Baugh and wide receiver Don Maynard, legendary football coach Gordon Wood and Masters champion Charles Coody were joined by Mindy Myers, that gutsy little girl from Munday who became the most decorated athlete in Texas high school history.

The Miracle Mavericks

As the 1982 Class 2A state football championship game was concluding at Baylor University's Floyd Casey Stadium in Waco, Rod Hess looked up to see an airplane flying overhead, pulling a red and black banner that read "Miracle Mavericks State Champions."

Indeed, it had been a miracle run for Hess and his Mavericks. Coaches love to talk about overcoming adversity and building character, but perhaps no state championship team dealt with more gut-wrenching, last-second drama and gave their fans more of a roller-coaster ride of emotions than the 1982 state champs from Eastland.

Hess, now retired and living in Leander, was the coach at Eastland during that remarkable season. But even he will admit there was little during the regular season to prepare his team and the Eastland fans for what they were about to face in the playoffs.

Eastland fans carried high hopes into the 1982 season, returning fourteen lettermen from an 11-2 team that lost in the quarterfinals to state champion Pilot Point a year earlier. Dave Campbell's *Texas Football* magazine had Eastland picked number two in the state in its preseason poll, and the Mavericks did little to disappoint their fans.

Through the first eleven weeks of the season, Eastland outscored its opponents 527-26, averaging nearly forty-eight points a game while allowing just slightly more than two points per contest.

Hess still remembers the only time Eastland trailed during the regular season. He calls it the most unusual play in his thirty-seven-year coaching career.

"Albany was supposed to be our toughest game in district," Hess recalled. "The game was in Albany, and we kicked off to them. On the third play of the game we got a defensive back (Jimmy Humphries) hurt. We didn't have trainers back then, so I walked out on the field to check on him. We helped him up to his feet. I got underneath one arm and I had one of the other defensive backs get under his other arm. We were walking him back to the sideline. We were still at the hash mark when I looked up. Albany was lined up in a swinging gate (an unusual spread formation) and they were running a play right at us."

Even though Hess and his injured player were still in the middle of the field, the officials had apparently blown the whistle to start play.

"I hollered at the other defensive back (who was helping the injured player off the field) to go make the tackle," Hess continued.

Albany scored on the play, however.

"As the ref ran by me, I grabbed his arm," Hess said. "He said, 'Coach, get off the field or I'll give you a fifteen-yard penalty.' I said something else to him, and he threw a flag. I kept walking Jimmy off the field, and then I turned around and said, 'You can't do that. It was an injury timeout,' and he threw another flag. My assistant Ronnie Hughes hollered at him, and he flagged him, too."

The Lions scored a two-point conversion to take the early 8-0 lead and then kicked off from Eastland's fifteen-yard line after the forty-five yards of penalties were stepped off against the Mavericks' coaches.

Despite the rough start, Eastland came back to win the game 41-8. "I've never seen a play like that before or since," said Hess, able to laugh about it years later. "After the game, (Albany coach) Tank Nelson said, 'I guess we made you mad.'"

In the second round of the playoffs, Eastland had to face Holliday in a rematch of the season opener that the Mavericks won 28-6. This time it was much different.

Eastland trailed for much of the game until quarterback Jay Hess, the coach's son, led the Mavericks on a fourth-quarter drive, hitting Thomas Sanders on a twenty-eight-yard touchdown pass. James Morton, now the head coach at Lubbock Monterey, kicked the extra point to tie the score 7-7.

Penetrations of the twenty-yard line and first downs, not overtime, were used to determine the outcome of tie games in those days, and Eastland led 2-1 in penetrations and also led in first downs. But this one wasn't over yet. Holliday intercepted a pass with 3:34 remaining and drove into Eastland's end of the field. With twelve seconds left, however, Holliday's thirty-three-yard field goal attempt into a strong south wind was wide, and the Mavericks were moving on to the third round.

On the way home from the game in Wichita Falls that night, however, four teenagers from Eastland—two boys who had been members of the 1981 team and two girls, one who was a senior and captain of the girls' basketball team—were killed in a car wreck near Graham.

The funerals for the four were held on Monday, and the team then played its next game—a rematch against Pilot Point—the following Thursday, Thanksgiving Day. Why was the game on Thursday?

When Hess met with Pilot Point coaches on that Saturday morning to set up the details of the game, he called back to the school where the team was watching film to see if it was all right to play that soon. The players' response was "the quicker the better."

Pilot Point brought a forty-two-game non-losing streak (forty-one wins and one tie) into the game, including an outright state championship in 1981 and a co-championship in 1980. It was also the last team to beat Eastland.

Pilot Point scored twice in the fourth quarter to take a 20-13 lead, the last touchdown coming with 2:20 remaining. Eastland got the ball on its own twenty-one after the kickoff.

"We were out of timeouts," Hess said. "Teams didn't work much on spread offenses in those days, so there was no way to communicate with the players."

Hess told his son that there was not enough time left to send in the plays, that he knew what to do. Jay Hess, who threw for 3,154 yards that season (a single-season state passing record at the time), engineered a seventy-nine-yard scoring drive in the final two minutes, completing five passes including one on third-and-four from the Eastland twenty-five and another on fourth-and-ten from the Pilot Point twenty-eight. Hess found Gary Stewart open for a nineteen-yard gain to the nine and then threw the ball away to stop the clock with twenty-three seconds left.

Hess hit Justin Owen with a touchdown pass in the end zone with eleven seconds to go, pulling the Mavericks to within one at 20-19. But Eastland had to go for two because Pilot Point led in penetrations. Hess and Owen hooked up again for a two-point conversion, giving Eastland the dramatic 21-20 victory, a victory made even more emotional by the funerals of the four teenagers just three days earlier.

"I really had nothing to do with that last drive," Hess said. "We didn't intend using tragedy for motivation, but I'm sure there was some motivation because the two boys who were killed had been members of the team a year earlier."

The next week, Eastland returned to Arlington to face Olney in the state quarterfinals. Trailing 29-21 with 11:58 to play, the Miracle Mavericks found a way to win another cliffhanger. Owen caught a tipped pass and turned it into a forty-one-yard scoring play. Morton, the team's fullback, ran it in for a two-point conversion, tying the score 29-29.

Karl Joiner then intercepted a pass, setting up Sanders' touchdown with 1:19 left, giving Eastland a 37-29 victory.

The Miracle Mavericks had one more thriller left in their emotional bag of tricks. Facing Hale Center in the rain and mud in the semifinals at Sweetwater's Mustang Bowl, Eastland trailed 12-9. But on fourth-and-thirteen with 1:23 to play, Hess threw a screen pass to Sanders, who turned it into a forty-one-yard touchdown and a 16-12 victory.

Four straight weeks and four straight victories—all decided in the final seconds—had put Eastland into the state championship game in Waco against East Bernard.

The title game was almost anticlimactic after what the Mavericks had put their fans through the previous month. Eastland breezed to a 28-6 victory and the amazing run was complete—except for the airplane and banner flying overhead that declared the "Miracle Mavericks State Champions."

It was a playoff run unlike any other.

You're Out of Here

··

It is not unusual for a basketball coach to get a technical and be ejected from a game after a disagreement with a referee, or a football coach be flagged for a 15-yard unsportsmanlike conduct penalty after protesting a call. An argument between a manager and an umpire in baseball occurs even more frequently and is often entertaining.

But how many times has a radio announcer or a public address announcer been kicked out of a game. Not very often, but it did happen to both Dave South and Dave Andrews, who now share more in common than just the same first name and a career in radio. They also hold the dubious distinction of both being kicked out of games in the most unusual—and humorous—of circumstances.

South, the long-time identifiable voice of Texas A&M sports on the radio, was ejected from a Southwest Conference basketball tournament game, while Andrews, a disc jockey at Rock 108 in Abilene at the time, was the public address announcer at a minor league baseball game when he was tossed for reading one of the team's sponsorship announcements during a game.

South's one-and-only run-in with a referee in his long broadcasting career occurred in the second half of a first-round game between Texas A&M and Houston in the 1993 SWC tournament at Reunion Arena in Dallas.

"The officiating in the first half was one-sided in favor of Houston," South recalled. "When the second half started, it was more of the same, against us and in favor of Houston. It seemed like the fouls were about two to one against us."

It was during a timeout in the second half that South "crossed paths" with official Brian Stout.

"With a three-man crew, one official is supposed to go to the baseline and look at one bench during a timeout," South said. "The second official is supposed to go to the other baseline and look at the other bench, and the third official is supposed to be at mid-court and look at the scorer's bench. If that would have happened, (the third official) would have had his back to me."

Instead, Stout walked to foul line and stared directly across at South, who was broadcasting the game from press row at courtside.

"I saw he was staring at me," South continued. "We weren't on the air because we were taking a commercial break. I looked over at (Houston coach) Pat Foster, and when I looked back Stout was still staring at me. So I smiled at him. With a soft drink in my right hand, I raised the soft drink and toasted him. I put my left hand on my throat (signifying the choke sign) for about two seconds. He immediately got a security guard and started screaming 'You're out of here, you're out of here.'"

A backdrop to the incident, according to South, was the fact that the *Houston Post* had done a story leading into the tournament about how bad the officiating had become in the Southwest Conference.

"One unnamed coach had been quoted in the story that he would rather have a dog call a game instead of Brian Stout," South said.

After the season, Stout and more than twenty other basketball officials, including the league's supervisor of officials Paul Galvan, lost their jobs with the SWC, according to South.

"I was just the straw that broke the camel's back," he added. "At the time, it was very embarrassing for me and the league."

A security guard escorted South off the floor to an elevator, and eventually to the front door in the lobby with the intentions of having him removed from Reunion Arena.

"I asked him to go get a Southwest Conference official because the referee only has control of the floor," South continued. "I asked them (the SWC officials) why I couldn't go back and do the postgame show when the game was over. After a long discussion, they said they would take me downstairs and lock me in a room—as if I was going to storm the court—until the game was over.

"Walking down the hallway to the room, I saw Tom Penders (the University of Texas coach) running toward me. We had never been formally introduced, but he knew I was the A&M announcer and I knew he was the Texas coach. He runs over, hugs me and whispers in my ear 'You're my new hero.'"

South said the incident took on a life of its own. It was on "SportsCenter" that night on ESPN. John Madden featured it on his national radio show. It made its own page on the "Sports Hall of Shame" calendar the next year, and the comic strip "Tank McNamara" did a whole week on the incident in which Tank gets kicked out by the referee.

"In fact, the two guys who do 'Tank McNamara' framed and autographed the original artwork and sent it to me," South said. "It is very funny now, and I tell the story all the time."

Twelve years later, South said he was standing outside the Texas A&M locker room waiting for Aggies coach Billy Gillispie at the Big 12 tournament at the American Airlines Center in Dallas when a security guard asked who he was.

"I'm with Texas A&M," South replied, and the security guard began telling him the story about the time the A&M radio announcer got kicked out of the game.

"I was the guy who escorted him out of the arena," the guard said.

"Well, you've got some of the story wrong," South told him.

"How do you know?" asked the guard.

"Because I was that radio announcer," South answered.

The guard immediately went to get one of his fellow guards so he could have his picture taken with South.

Dave Andrews was a disc jockey at a rock station in Abilene in 1995, but he won a contest to become the public address announcer for the inaugural minor league baseball season of the Abilene Prairie Dogs in the now defunct independent Texas-Louisiana League.

"The Prairie Dogs were playing the Amarillo Dillas," Andrews recalled. "It was late in the game, and we were down by six runs. We had a guy on second, and our batter hit a shot down the line. All of us in the press box and everyone in the crowd thought it was fair, but the umpire called it foul. (Abilene manager) Charley Kerfeld (the former Houston Astros relief pitcher) came out to argue. Well, he got tossed. The argument went on for quite awhile, and he eventually threw bats and gloves out of the dugout and on to the field."

Let's just say Kerfeld wasn't deleting any expletives in his argument with the umpires, so team officials in the press box told Andrews to read some announcements to help drown out Kerfeld's vociferous tirade against the umpires.

"Before Charley left the field, he took off his glasses and shook them at the umpire," Andrews continued. "I had read all of the other announcements, so then I read the announcement about our promotion that night: 'Ladies and gentleman, the Abilene Prairie Dogs want to thank Lenscrafters for sponsoring Sunglasses Night.' I had read the same announcement three times earlier in the game."

This time, however, both umpires, Vince Price and Mel Chittum, turned toward the press box and immediately signaled that Andrews had been kicked out of the game. They wouldn't resume the game until Andrews left the press box.

A week later, the Prairie Dogs and Lubbock Crickets got into a brawl in Lubbock, and Chittum kicked Jimmy Cricket, Lubbock's mascot, out of the game. The ejections of a public address announcer and a mascot were featured in *Sports Illustrated*.

But Andrews got the last laugh out of the incident.

"The next day, I knocked on their dressing room door before the game and asked if I could have my picture taken with them," Andrews chuckled.

His radio station also sponsored a "You're out of here" promotion. Every time listeners heard an umpire say "You're out of here," on the air, the radio station took the eighth caller and put the listener's name into a drawing for a "You're out of here" trip and shopping spree in Dallas.

Andrews, just like the players and coaches in the league, was fined fifty dollars for his ejection. The Prairie Dogs' fans and radio station listeners donated more than $500 to Andrews, however, so he called the league office to ask what they did with the money when players paid fines. Told the league gave it to charity, Andrews asked if he could give the money he had received to the charity of his choice.

The league said that would be OK, so Andrews said he donated the money—to the Lighthouse Foundation for the Blind—in the names of the two umpires.

The Greatest Sprinter of All Time

In October 2006, San Benito High School, located in the Rio Grande Valley, named its new 11,000-seat football stadium Bobby Morrow Stadium in honor of a former San Benito football player. Morrow, now a farmer near his hometown, was on hand for the stadium dedication.

Former Abilene Christian sprinter Bobby Morrow won three gold medals at the 1956 Olympic games in Melbourne, Australia, and has been lauded by many as the greatest sprinter of all time. Courtesy Abilene Christian University Creative Services.

But it was all the way across the state and halfway around the world where Morrow became known as "the greatest sprinter of all time."

When I first came to Abilene, Texas, to interview for a new job, there was only one thing I knew about Abilene. That was where Bobby Morrow had run track, at Abilene Christian College. I can still picture Morrow on the cover of *Sports Illustrated, Sport* and *Life* magazines, wearing his ACC jersey.

What I didn't know at the time was that Abilene

Christian had assembled perhaps the most amazing group of sprinters at one school in the history of track and field during the time Morrow ran for the Wildcats. Eleven of the twelve ACU athletes who set twelve world records from 1956-1961, along with their coaches Oliver Jackson and Bill McClure, returned to the Abilene campus more than forty years later for an interview with freelance writer Mike Shropshire and a *Sports Illustrated* photographer for a retrospective feature on their remarkable era.

"There were only 1,900 students at Abilene Christian then," ACU president Royce Money said in making a presentation to the legendary track stars during the school's chapel ceremony. "They put Abilene Christian and Abilene on the map. They helped build the foundation for ACU athletics."

It certainly wasn't the facilities in Abilene that attracted Morrow and the other great sprinters.

"When I was here, we had a dirt track that went uphill in some places and downhill in other places," Morrow recalled

No matter. By his sophomore year, Morrow had tied world records in the 100- and 200-meter dashes.

"Bobby had a fluidity of motion like nothing I'd ever seen," Jackson told the *Sports Illustrated* writer. "He could run a 220 with a root beer float on his head and never spill a drop. I made an adjustment to his start when Bobby was a freshman. After that, my only advice to him was to change his major from ag sciences to speech, because he'd be destined to make a bunch of them."

But how would Morrow fare away from windy West Texas against the best the world had to offer? In the 1956 Olympics in Melbourne, Australia, he won the 100 meters. Then he led an American sweep of the medals in the 200, equaling the Olympic record. He followed that by anchoring the American 4x100 relay to a gold medal and a world record.

Morrow was the first American to win the 100 and 200 at the Olympics since Jesse Owens in 1936. No one other than Carl Lewis in 1984 has done it since.

"I was standing near the finish line for the 100-meter finals in Melbourne," Olympic pole vault gold medalist Bob Richards said in *Sports Illustrated*. "The track was terrible. Loose, like sawdust, and Bobby was kicking cinders 10 feet into the air behind him.

On a modern surface, there is no doubt in my mind that Bobby would have run an eight-something 100 meters. He was the greatest sprinter I ever saw."

When Morrow returned from Australia, he not only was featured on the cover of all of the nation's top magazines but he also appeared on the Ed Sullivan Show and won the James E. Sullivan Award as the nation's top amateur athlete.

Abilene Christian's 440-yard relay team of (from left) Waymond Griggs, Bill Woodhouse, James Segrest and Bobby Morrow set four world records. Segrest and Morrow are members of the Texas Sports Hall of Fame. Courtesy Abilene Christian University Creative Services.

After retiring from track, he returned to the farm in San Benito where he lives today in relative anonymity.

It is incredible to think of the collection of sprinters the small Abilene school assembled during that time. From 1956-1961, Abilene Christian runners set world records in the 4x100 relay, 4x200 relay, 100-yard dash, 100-meter dash and 200-meter dash. In 1959, Bill Woodhouse tied Morrow's 1957 world record time of 9.3 in the 100-yard dash during a meet at ACU's Elmer Gray Stadium.

How did such an amazing group of athletes come to Abilene Christian at the same time?

"I don't know," Morrow admitted. "Most of the competition came from each other. But the guys got along. We enjoyed traveling together and working out together. Egos weren't a problem. Give credit to Coach Jackson. He didn't have to say anything. He'd just look at us and we'd know what he meant.

Morrow, Woodhouse, Don Conder, Calvin Cooley, Waymond Griggs, George Peterson, Dennis Richardson, James Segrest and Earl Young, who helped ACU relay teams set five world records, returned for the 1999 reunion. The other relay member, Bud Clanton, is deceased. Young won a gold medal at the 1960 Olympic Games in Rome as a member of the U.S. 4x400 relay team.

The Abilene Christian track program, led by Jackson, was held in such high regard that the U.S. Olympic Committee held its 1960 women's Olympic Trials in Abilene. The star of the trials was Wilma Rudolph, who went on to win gold medals in the 100, 200 and 4x100 relay in Rome, becoming the first woman to win three gold medals in the Olympic Games.

No doubt, there was something about sprinters running in Abilene during that era.

Hall of Fame pitcher Nolan Ryan (left), Olympic gold medalist Bobby Morrow (right) and PGA Tour legend Byron Nelson (seated) gathered in Abilene on May 28, 2005, to take part in ACU's Centennial Champions luncheon where each was honored for his contribution to ACU athletics. Morrow was named ACU's Athlete of the Century at the luncheon, while Ryan and Nelson were each hailed for helping ACU baseball and men's golf programs, respectively. It's believed that this is the only photograph these three Texas legends have ever taken together. Courtesy of Abilene Christian University Creative Services.

One for the Ages

This story is one most Texans have heard, but most don't know all of the story.

Plano East had just scored a touchdown to go in front of Tyler John Tyler 44-41 with twenty-four seconds remaining on the Texas Stadium clock in their 1994 Class 5A playoff football game when Tyler quarterback Morris Anderson approached head coach Allen Wilson on the sideline.

"Don't worry, Coach, we've got this one," Anderson told his coach.

"I turned to one of my assistants," Wilson recalled, "and asked, 'What is he smoking?'"

Quite frankly, the fans still remaining—most had left earlier, thinking the game was over—for the third game of a playoff tripleheader on that November evening at Texas Stadium in Irving were also probably wondering if they were smoking an hallucinogenic substance as they watched the final moments of the most improbable finish in Texas high school football history.

Ask a hundred football fans to name the greatest high school football game they've ever seen, and you will likely get a hundred different answers. But ask a hundred knowledgeable fans to name the wildest, wackiest finish in a high school football game, and the answer might be unanimous: the Plano East-John Tyler playoff game in 1994.

Even ask a football fan outside the Lone Star State that same question, and you'll likely get the same answer. The finish of the Plano East-John Tyler game was shown on ESPN, the announcers on the Plano broadcast were invited to appear on the Tonight

Show, and the two schools involved became the first high schools to win an ESPY Award for the greatest game of 1994.

"I still get asked about it all the time, when they find out who I am," said Wilson, now the head coach at Dallas Carter High School. "Even people outside of the state of Texas want to talk about it."

The story about how this game became the most well-known, talked-about high school football game ever is almost as interesting as the game itself.

"Long after you and I are gone, they'll be talking about this game," said Eddy Clinton, who was the play-by-play announcer on the taped replay telecast of the game for the Plano Independent School District channel on the Plano cable system.

Before you find out how their call of the game landed Clinton and his partner in the broadcast booth a spot on the Tonight Show with Jay Leno, let's set the stage for the game itself. Both teams were 12-0 going into their third-round showdown, and the game was a good one. But who could imagine what was about to unfold as time wound down in the fourth quarter? Six touchdowns in the final 3:03 turned a good high school playoff football game into a classic, one for the ages.

John Tyler was leading 27-17, but Plano East was driving for an apparent score when a John Tyler defender stripped the ball away from quarterback Jeff Whitley and returned it ninety-two yards for a touchdown. Moments later, Plano East fumbled again, and David Warren scooped it up and raced thirty-five yards for a touchdown. A close game had seemingly turned into a rout as John Tyler led 41-17 with only 3:03 remaining.

Someone forgot to tell Plano East that the game was over, however. Whitley guided the Panthers to a quick score, cutting the deficit to 41-23.

Plano East then recovered an onside kick with 2:24 to go.

"After the first one, I didn't think much about it," Wilson continued. "All we needed to do was recover the kick and go home."

Whitley hit John Braddock with a touchdown pass, and the Panthers converted a two-point conversion, trimming John Tyler's lead to 41-31 with 1:30 left.

"Before the next onside kick, we told our kids to wait on the ball, to make sure it went ten yards," Wilson said. "But Roderick Dunn attacked the ball."

Dunn, a starting free safety for the Lions, jumped out to grab the bouncing ball. The kick caromed off him, and Plano East recovered. Whitley and Braddock then hooked up on another quick score, and suddenly it was 41-37.

Now this was starting to get a little scary for Wilson and the Lions. Plano East tried another onside kick, and recovered it when Dunn fumbled it again with forty-nine seconds to go. Three perfectly executed onside kicks, and Plano East fans were beginning to believe in miracles.

The Panthers scored again, this time with just twenty-four seconds to go, taking an improbable 44-41 lead. In a span of 2:12, Plano East had scored twenty-seven points. As Wilson gathered his shell-shocked team around him, he fully expected another onside kick from his opponent.

"It is amazing to try three and get all three," he said. "We thought they'd kick a fourth one. Really, we were in our onside kick situation."

"I was celebrating when I saw they had nine men on the line of scrimmage," Plano East coach Scott Smith, who admitted he first considered a short pooch kick before his assistants talked him into kicking deep. "I knew Terrence Green would kick it over their heads."

Wilson did make one change in his kick return alignment. He took Dunn, the goat on the two previous onside kicks, off the front line and put him back at the twenty-yard line in case Plano East tried a short kick.

Instead, the Panthers kicked it deep. As the ball sailed over Dunn's head, he raced back, caught it at the three-yard line and then started up the left sideline.

"Plano East's kids were well-coached," Wilson said. "They had been taught to run in their lanes going down the field, only they didn't get out of their lanes. Dunn ran right past them. David Warren was running alongside of him, looking around for someone to block. I was afraid he was going to knock Dunn out-of-bounds."

Dunn raced ninety-seven yards untouched for a touchdown, scoring with eleven seconds left to help John Tyler claim an amazing 48-44 victory. In just 2:52, the score had changed from 41-17 to 48-44.

"You'll never see another finish that dramatic," said Wilson, whose John Tyler team went on to win the state championship that year. "Plano East should have quit when we went ahead 41-17, but they kept scoring. You have to take your hat off to their kids. But when you got down, you'd think our kids would have hung their head. But our kids didn't quit, either. The way the game ended was mind-boggling."

Equally as mind-boggling is the attention the three announcers received. Clinton, who had dabbled in broadcasting and now owns a billboard business, and Denny Garver, a mailman in Plano, had handled the telecasts of the Plano I.S.D. games free of charge for ten years, calling the games for replay on the Plano cable system. In fact, they did all three games of the playoff tripleheader that day at Texas Stadium. In the final game, they invited Mike Zuffoto, the head coach at Richardson Lake Highlands, to join them.

Clinton admitted they weren't the normal professional announcers, instead having fun with their country style during the telecasts and openly pulling for the Plano teams to win.

"The game was the third game of the day, so it didn't start until nearly nine o'clock that night," Clinton recalled. "All the affiliates (the Dallas television stations) left at ten o'clock. Of course, everyone thought the game was over."

The next morning, Clinton said Scott Murray of the NBC affiliate in Dallas called the Plano cable company to ask if he could get a copy of the telecast.

"This was an unbelievable game," Murray said in the opening to his sports show Sunday night, "and wait till you hear the idiots doing the game."

Murray sent the feed of his story to the NBC network, and the local announcers' lives were never the same again.

The next day, Jay Leno called Clinton to see if the announcers would appear on the Tonight Show.

"Send us a cab and a case of Lone Star, and we'll be there," Clinton told the entertainer.

"I know what a cab is, but what is Lone Star?" Leno asked.

Clinton explained it was a Texas beer. Leno then flew the two to Burbank, set them up for four days in California and even had four cases of Lone Star beer flown in from San Antonio.

"It was fun," Clinton said, "and (Leno) was fabulous."

Their broadcast was the lead story on "SportsCenter" on ESPN for several days and the game won an ESPY Award as the top game of 1994, the only high school game to ever receive an ESPY. ESPN2 did an anniversary feature on the game ten years later. The story of the game appeared in *Sports Illustrated*. Clinton and Garver even landed a role as the hometown announcers for the West Caanan Coyotes in the movie *Varsity Blues*.

It was Zuffoto, however, who uttered the most famous line of the broadcast.

"No, no, I don't believe it," Zuffoto cried as Dunn broke into the clear and raced down the left sideline for the winning touchdown. "God bless those kids. I'm sick. I'm gonna to throw up."

It was an unforgettable call to the finish of an unbelievable game.

"This was like Bobby Thompson's home run in 1951," Clinton said. "There have been great games since then. It was just a combination of a great game and the way we did it. It hit nationwide, and we caught lightning in a bottle."

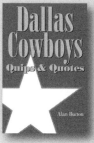